Skeleton French

All you need to build up your body of French grammar!

Claire Buet-Charlwood and David Mort

GALORE PARK

Published by Galore Park Publishing Ltd
338 Euston Road, London NW1 3BH
www.galorepark.co.uk

Text copyright © Claire Buet-Charlwood and David Mort 2004
Illustrations copyright © Galore Park 2004

Illustrations by Mike Sparrow: www.mikesparrow.com

The right of Claire Buet-Charlwood and David Mort to be identified as the authors of this work
has been asserted by them in accordance with sections 77 and 78 of the Copyright, Designs
and Patents Act 1988.

Printed by Charlesworth Press, Wakefield

ISBN 13: 978 1 902984 61 2

First published 2004
Re-printed 2007, 2010, 2014

Acknowledgements

Claire Buet-Charlwood and David Mort would like to thank their respective spouses –
or should that be spice? – Mark and Linda, for their constant support and cups of undrunk
coffee while they beavered away. Many thanks also to Nick Oulton, whose genial editorial
genius has brought the Skeleton to life.

Contents

Part One: The Bare Bones

1. **A sentence**: What is it and how does it work? — 2
2. **Nouns**: Male or female? One, or more than one? — 4
3. **Articles**: How to say 'the', 'a', 'an' and 'some' — 6
4. **Adjectives**: Great! cool! wicked! — 8
5. **The present tense**: 'I'm doing it now!' — 11
6. **The future tense**: 'I'm going to …' — 16
7. **Accents**: Be 'acute': avoid 'grave' mistakes! — 17
8. **The past tense**: 'I've done it!' — 19
9. **Question time**: Who? Where? When? How? What? How many? Why? How long? How much? Which? — 22
10. **Negatives**: It's not a problem! — 24
11. **Prepositions**: From me to you! — 25
12. **Pronouns**: French grammar? It's easy! — 29

Part Two: Body Building

13. **More squiggles**: The 'fish hook' and the 'two funny dots' : what are they for? — 32
14. **Masculine or feminine?**: More tips about the gender of nouns — 34
15. **Adjectives**: Before or after the noun? More about agreements, and how to make comparisons — 39
16. **More adjectives**: Demonstrative and possessive adjectives: this book is my property! — 45
17. **Adverbs**: Understand French grammar easily! — 48
18. **Reflexive verbs**: Help yourself! — 50
19. **More about the present tense**: More about verbs, regular and irregular — 52
20. **More about the future tense**: It will be easy! — 57
21. **More about the perfect tense**: Past participles — 60
22. **Still more about the perfect tense!**: Verbs that take *être* — 62
23. **The imperfect tense**: Why another past tense? — 65
24. **More about questions**: Are there other ways to ask them? — 67
25. **More about negatives**: 'Never', 'nobody', 'no more', 'nothing' and 'only' — 71
26. **More about pronouns**: A host of new pronouns — 73

Practice Exercises — 79

Skeleton Key: Answers to the exercises — 109

Part One: The Bare Bones

Chapter 1:   A sentence

What is it and how does it work?

A **sentence** is a group of words working together, like people in an organisation. Some have more responsibility than others. The two main kinds of words are **verbs** and **nouns**.

Verbs

Verbs say what 'happens' or what 'is'; they are 'doing' or 'being' words.

Examples:			
manger	to eat	*aller*	to go
dormir	to sleep	*parler*	to speak
travailler	to work	*exister*	to exist
avoir	to have	*devenir*	to become

For a sentence to be a sentence, it must always contain a verb.

☺ As in English, a pause in a sentence is shown by a **comma** (,). The end of a sentence is shown by a **full stop** (.), an **exclamation mark** (!) or a **question mark** (?). The first word of a sentence starts with a **capital letter**.

Examples:	
Vous avez soif?	Are you thirsty?
Voulez-vous un café, ou un thé?	Do you want a coffee, or a tea?
Moi, j'aime mieux le coca.	I prefer Coke myself.

Nouns

Nouns are the names of things, animals, people or places.

Examples:			
chaise	chair	*magasin*	shop
girafe	giraffe	*moustique*	mosquito
directeur	headmaster	*oncle*	uncle
Londres	London		

Nouns written with a capital letter are called **proper nouns**.

Examples:			
Marie	Mary	*Frédéric*	Frederic
Paris	Paris	*Alpes*	Alps

☺ Words that are proper nouns in English are nearly always proper nouns in French as well. There are a small number of exceptions, such as the names of days, months and languages, which do not begin with a capital letter.

Examples:

mardi	Tuesday
mai	May
le français	French (language)

Practice 1.1

Other parts of speech

A noun is often accompanied by:
(i) an **article** (to act as its bodyguard):

Examples:

le, la	the	*un, une*	a/an

(ii) a **preposition** (to introduce it):

Examples:

après	after	*dans*	in
avec	with	*à*	at/to

(iii) an **adjective** (to describe it):

Examples:

grand	big	*vieux*	old
bleu	blue	*notre*	our

A noun can be replaced by a **pronoun** (to avoid repetition):

Examples:

il	he	*les*	them
vous	you		

You can use a **conjunction** (to link ideas):

Examples:

et	and	*ou*	or
mais	but		

A verb or an adjective can be accompanied by an **adverb** (to describe it):

Examples:

facilement	easily	*bien*	well

Practice 1.2 to 1.4

These parts can work together to form a sentence:
Le village s'appelle Gilly. Il est petit et normalement calme. Il est situé sur la Nationale 6, avant Albertville.

The village is called Gilly. It is small and normally quiet. It is situated on the A6, before Albertville.

s'appelle, est, est situé are verbs;
village is a noun;
Gilly, Nationale 6, Albertville are proper nouns;
le, la are articles;
sur, avant are prepositions;
petit, calme are adjectives;
il is a pronoun;
et is a conjunction;
normalement is an adverb.

Chapter 2: | Nouns

Male or female? One, or more than one?

A **noun** is the name of a thing, animal, person or place (see Chapter 1, page 2). In French, all nouns are either male (**masculine**) or female (**feminine**). Masculine and feminine refer to the **gender** of a noun. This also happens in other languages which, like French, have come from Latin. It explains why, in Spanish and Italian, nouns have mostly the same genders as in French.

English has masculine and feminine for living creatures, and all other nouns are neuter ('it') - although sailors refer to their boats as 'she'. French has no neuter: everything is a 'he' or a 'she'.

Even the French can't always know for sure whether a noun is masculine or feminine. With a word they have not seen before, they make it masculine or feminine according to the gender of words with which it rhymes. That works well most of the time, but sometimes even they make mistakes!

Examples:			
Feminine	*bague*	ring	
Feminine	*vague*	wave	
so:	*blague*	joke	is likely to be feminine too (and it is!).

Of course, the best way of knowing for certain is to check in a dictionary.

Masculine or feminine?

One thing is easy: a noun is almost certainly masculine if it ends with a consonant, except if the consonant is in the ending '**–ion**', in which case it is almost certainly feminine.

Le mot **chemise** est féminin et **chemisier** masculin. Pourquoi?

The word '**shirt**' is feminine and '**blouse**' masculine. Why?

Examples:					
Masculine	*le championnat*	the championship	**Feminine**	*la division*	the division
	le match	the match		*une compétition*	a competition
	le Portugal	Portugal	but ☠		
	un joueur	a player	**Masculine**	*un avion*	an aeroplane
	un ballon	a football		*un champion*	a champion

☠ However, the gender of nouns ending in a vowel is not always so predictable! To find out more about genders, see Chapter 14, page 34.

📖 Practice 2.1

Singular or plural?

Singular refers to 'one', **plural** refers to 'more than one'. In French as in English, to show there is more than one noun, you normally add an '**s**' on the end of the noun, but in French, the '**s**' is not normally heard.

Examples:

Singular		Plural	
un croissant	a croissant	*des croissants*	(some) croissants
une limonade	a lemonade	*deux limonades*	two lemonades
le biscuit	the biscuit	*les biscuits*	the biscuits

Practice 2.2

Unusual plural endings

Noah: All aboard! One mouse or two mouses? One sheep or two sheeps? One horse or two horses? One child or two childs?

Some words in French, just as in English, have a different ending when they are plural. So, just as 'mouse' becomes 'mice', 'sheep' stays as 'sheep', and 'child' becomes 'children', the plural form of some French words just has to be learnt!

Most nouns ending in '*–al*' change to '*–aux*'
Most nouns ending in '*–au*' and '*–eu*' add '*–x*' instead of '*-s*'
☺ Good news! Nouns ending in '*–s*' or '*–z*' do not change when they are plural.

> Tous à bord! Une souri**s** ou deux souri**s**? Un mouton ou deux mouton**s**? Un cheval ou deux chev**aux**? Un enfant ou deux enfant**s**?

Examples:

Singular		Plural	
une souris	a mouse	*cent souris*	one hundred mice
un nez	a nose	*cent nez*	one hundred noses
le journal	the newspaper	*les journaux*	the newspapers
un cadeau	a gift	*dix cadeaux*	ten gifts
le jeu	the game	*les jeux*	the games

Practice 2.3

Unusual pronunciations

Some nouns seem to have a mind (or a pronunciation) of their own!

Examples:

Singular		Plural
un_œuf (rhymes with *neuf*=nine)	an egg	*des_œufs* (rhymes with *deux*=two)
un bœuf (as above)	an ox	*des bœufs* (as above)

It is rather like: 'one w**o**man' – 'two w**o**men' in English! Notice that we sometimes put an 'underscore' mark to show that two words run together (e.g. *des_oeufs*)

> Why did the French waiter say: '***Deux oeufs***? *Non, désolé*?'
> Because ***un oeuf*** is **enough**!

Chapter 3: Articles

How to say 'the', 'a', 'an' and 'some'

Remember? An **article** acts as bodyguard to a noun (see Chapter 1, page 3). In English, as in French, there are two kinds of articles: indefinite and definite. But in French, because all nouns are either masculine or feminine, there are more forms to learn.

Indefinite articles

Indefinite articles accompany nouns that are **not defined**. In the singular we use 'a' (or 'an'); in the plural we use 'some':

> '**a** bus' (i.e. any bus, not a particular one)
> '**an** elephant' (i.e. any elephant)
> '**some** shops' (i.e. any shops)

Tu peux me passer un livre de grammaire française, s'il te plaît? Non, pas ça! Je veux dire le chouette livre avec les dessins!

In French if the noun is masculine singular, we use **un**:

Examples:	
un bus	a bus
un_éléphant	an elephant

'Can you pass me **a** French grammar book please? No! not that one . I mean **the** cool book with **the** pictures!'

If the noun is feminine singular, we use **une**:

Examples:	
une voiture	a car
une orange	an orange

The '–n' of **un** is not pronounced, except when it comes before a vowel sound. It then acts as a linking sound (*un_acrobate*, *un_animal*), just as, in English, '**a**' becomes '**an**' before a vowel sound to make it easier to say (e.g. an elephant, an orange).

If the noun is plural, we use **des**:

Examples:	
des boutiques	some shops
des_ordinateurs	some computers

Note that the '–s' of **des** is not pronounced, except when it comes before a vowel. It then acts as a linking sound (*des_ordinateurs*, *des_éléphants*).
Important! In English, '**some**' is often missed out, but you cannot miss out **des** before the noun in French.
e.g. *des_ordinateurs* = 'some computers' or just 'computers'.

To find out more about how to say 'some' in French, see Chapter 11, page 27.

Practice 3.1

Definite articles:

Definite articles accompany nouns that are defined. We use the definite article when we are referring to a particular noun. In English, for singular and plural, we use 'the':

> 'the bus' (e.g. 'bus number 192')
> 'the elephant' (e.g. 'Nelly the elephant')
> 'the shops' (e.g. 'the shops near my house')

If the noun is masculine singular, we use *le*:

Examples:
le bus   the bus

If the noun is feminine singular, we use *la*:

Examples:
la famille   the family

If the noun is plural, we use *les*:

Examples:
les_ordinateurs   the computers
les boutiques   the shops

As with *des*, the '*s*' of *les* is not pronounced,
except when it comes before a vowel sound to act as a linking sound (*les_ordinateurs*, *les_éléphants*).

In French, *les* can be used to mean 'any kind of' something. In English no article is used in this situation.

Example:
I like carrots but not mushrooms.   *J'aime **les** carottes mais pas **les** champignons.*

Before any noun beginning with a vowel sound, *le* or *la* shorten to *l'*. This makes it easier to say.

Examples:
l'éléphant   the elephant
(the *le* is truncated!)
l'hôtel   the hotel
l'histoire   the story

Practice 3.2

I've been truncated!

Note: '*h*' in French is usually seen but not heard, like '*k*' in English (as in 'knock') and sometimes '*h*' (as in 'honest'). This means that a word beginning with '*h*' starts with a vowel sound, so you use the '*n*' of *un* as a link when you say it.
You say *l'* instead of *le* or *la*, and use the '*s*' of *des* and *les* as a link when you say it.

Examples:
un_(h)ôtel = a hotel, *l'(h)ôtel* = the hotel, *des_(h)ôtels* = some hotels, *les_(h)ôtels* = the hotels.
une_(h)istoire = a story, *l'(h)istoire* = the story, *des_(h)istoires* = some stories,
les_(h)istoires = the stories.

Chapter 4 | Adjectives

CD 9

Great! Cool! Wicked!

French noun: 'Mr Adjective, do you understand? You must do exactly as I said!'
French adjective: 'Yes sir, anything you say sir, I totally agree!'

> M. Adjectif, vous comprenez? Vous devez faire exactement ce que je vous ai dit!

> Oui monsieur, très bien, monsieur, je suis entièrement d'accord!

Remember? An **adjective** acts as an assistant to a noun, describing it (see Chapter 1, page 3).

Feminine agreement of adjectives

French nouns are more influential than English nouns. They force their adjectives to become masculine or feminine, singular or plural, to match (or **agree** with) them.

When the adjective describes a masculine singular noun, it is in its shortest form (the one you'll find in a dictionary). With a feminine singular noun, the adjective adds an '–*e*'. If it already ends with '–*e*', it stays the same.

Examples:

Masculine		Feminine	
un petit sac	a small bag	*une petite jupe*	a little skirt
le pull uni	the plain jumper	*la chemise unie*	the plain shirt
l'uniforme orange	the orange uniform	*la cravate orange*	the orange tie

The feminine '*e*' is not heard, but it causes a consonant before it to be heard (*intéressant* ⇒ *intéressante*). This is similar to the 'magic '*e*'' in English, which causes letters before it to be pronounced differently (bit ⇒ bite, con ⇒ cone).

 Practice. 4.1

CD 10

Plural agreement of adjectives

Most **adjectives** describing a **masculine plural** noun add an '–*s*'. If they already end with an '–*s*', they stay the same. With a **feminine plural** noun, the **adjective** adds an '–*s*' to the feminine singular form.

Examples:

Singular		Plural	
un chemisier noir	a black blouse	*trois chemisiers noirs*	three black blouses
une jupe noire	a black skirt	*deux jupes noires*	two black skirts
le pull gris	the grey jumper	*les pulls gris*	the grey jumpers
la chemise grise	the grey shirt	*les chemises grises*	the grey shirts
la cravate orange	the orange tie	*les cravates oranges*	the orange ties

Practice 4.2

☸ **Two things to note:**

1. You will notice a few adjectives not behaving exactly as shown above, but using slightly different endings. These need to be learned by heart.

2. English adjectives always come **before** their noun. Most French adjectives come **after** their noun. Some come before, but this is rare.

Examples:

un prix exceptionnel	an exceptional price
une promotion exceptionnelle	an exceptional promotion
le beau costume	the beautiful suit
les beaux costumes	the beautiful suits
la belle robe	the beautiful dress
les belles robes	the beautiful dresses

To find out more about the position of adjectives, see Chapter 15, page 39, and for more about irregular adjectives, see Chapter 15, page 41.

D 1

Possessive adjectives

Possessive adjectives show what belongs to which owner. Like other French adjectives, they agree with the noun they describe. Remember, though, that the focus is not on the owner, as it is in English, but on the person or thing possessed. In other words, when deciding which version of the word for 'my' to use (**mon**, **ma** or **mes**), it is the noun being possessed that is significant, not who is doing the possessing. Look carefully at the following examples:

Mon père est drôlement possessif. Si **ma** sœur ou **mes** frères sortent seuls, il est furieux!

'**My** father is really possessive. If **my** sister or **my** brothers go out on their own, he is furious!'

How to translate 'my':

my	
+ masculine singular noun	**mon** *lit* – **my** bed
+ feminine singular noun	**ma** *maison* – **my** house
+ plural noun	**mes** *vêtements* – **my** clothes

Practice 4.3

How to translate 'your':

your	
+ masculine singular noun	**ton** *lit* – **your** bed
+ feminine singular noun	**ta** *maison* – **your** house
+ plural noun	**tes** *vêtements* – **your** clothes

Practice 4.4

How to translate 'his', 'her', 'its':

his	her	its
+ masculine singular noun		
son lit – his bed	*son* lit – her bed	*son* lit – its bed
+ feminine singular noun		
sa maison – his house	*sa* maison – her house	*sa* maison – its house
+ plural noun		
ses vêtements – his clothes	*ses* vêtements – her clothes	*ses* vêtements – its clothes

Practice 4.5

So, for each possessive word in English, there is a choice of words in French.

my	*mon* + masculine singular noun
	ma + feminine singular noun
	mes + plural noun
your	*ton* + masculine singular noun
	ta + feminine singular noun
	tes + plural noun
his, her, its	*son* + masculine singular noun
	sa + feminine singular noun
	ses + plural noun

Remember: the focus is not on the owner in French, but on the person or thing possessed.

To find out more about possessive adjectives, see Chapter 16, pages 46 and 47.

Practice 4.6

Chapter 5:   The present tense

I'm doing it now!

Remember, the verb is the most important word – the 'boss' of a sentence.

The present tense

The word **tense** refers to the time when something happens. As in English, there are three main tenses or time frames: past, present and future.

The **present tense** is used to talk about what is happening now, and what is generally true.

> **Examples:**
> *Aujourd'hui je suis chez moi.*   Today I am at home.
> *Je regarde la télé.*   I am watching the telly.
> *C'est une émission sur la Terre.*   It is a programme about the Earth.
> *La Terre est une planète.*   The Earth is a planet.

Categories of verbs

French verbs come in three main categories, called **–er** verbs, **–ir** verbs and **–re** verbs. This is how their **infinitive** form ends (the **infinitive** is the form found in the dictionary). The **infinitive** does not tell you when something is going on (tenses do that), but means 'to …' e.g. 'to speak', 'to sell', 'to finish'.

Most verbs (about 90%) are from the **–er** category. That is approximately 4000 verbs!

☺ The really good thing about **–er** verbs is that they all follow the same pattern (except one: *aller*, and a few others with spelling oddities). To find out more about these, see Chapter 7, page 18, and Chapter 13, page 33.

The present tense of –er verbs

French verbs have different **endings** depending on who does the action. They are presented in a specific order, called a **conjugation**. You will find things easier if you learn how to set out verbs properly, and what the various parts are called, so have a look at the verb *jouer* (to play) in French:

> *jouer* = **to play**
>
> | | **Singular** | | **Plural** | |
> |---|---|---|---|---|
> | 1st person | *je joue* | I play | *nous jouons* | we play |
> | 2nd person | *tu joues* | you play | *vous jouez* | you play |
> | 3rd person | *il/elle/on joue* | he/she/one plays | *ils/elles jouent* | they play |

Six things to note:

1. The French endings shown in bold *replace* the *–er* of the infinitive.

2. 'I play' and 'I am playing' are the same in French (two for the price of one!).

3. There is no special word for 'it'; everything is either 'he' or 'she'.

4. When meaning 'people **generally**', the 3rd person singular form with *on* is often used in French. Literally *on joue* means 'one plays' but *on* is used much more than 'one' in English. It is equivalent to 'we play / you play / they play', when these do not refer to any specific people. For this reason, *on* is called an **impersonal** word.

5. There are two ways of saying 'you' in French: *tu* when speaking to one person in a familiar way (a friend, a relative, a pet, someone you are shouting rude words at!), *vous* when you have to be respectful or formal, or when you are addressing more than one person.

6. There are two ways of saying 'they' in French: *elles* is for feminine only, whereas *ils* is used for masculine or a mixed group of masculine and feminine.

There are three things you can hear:

1. The verb endings for *je, tu, il, elle, on, ils, elles* all have the same sound.

2. *je* is shortened to *j'* before a vowel sound, to make it easier to say: e.g. *j'adore*.

3. The '*–s*' of *nous, vous, ils, elles* and the '*–n*' of *on* are used as a linking sound before a vowel sound, to make it easier to say: e.g. *nous_adorons, vous_adorez, ils_adorent, elles_adorent, on_adore.* In front of a consonant, they are not heard: e.g. *nous parlons, vous parlez, ils parlent, elles parlent, on parle.*

Maintenant **ils** habitent sur une île déserte!
'Now **they** live on a desert island!'

Practice 5.1 and 5.2

☺☺ So, in just a few minutes, you have learnt how to use 4000 French verbs! These are called **regular** verbs because they all follow the same pattern.

☺ Not only that, but you will see that other French verbs (called *–ir* verbs and *–re* verbs) have endings that work in a similar way.

To find out more about regular *–ir* and *–re* verbs, see Chapter 19, pages 52 and 55.

Irregular verbs

☠ Some verbs do not follow the same pattern. These are called **irregular** verbs. Let's look at five very useful ones:

1. être

'**To be** or not **to be**, that is the question!'
Etre *ou ne pas* ***être****, telle est la question!*

être **= to be**

	Singular		Plural	
1st person	*je suis*	I am	*nous sommes*	we are
2nd person	*tu es*	you are	*vous êtes*	you are
3rd person	*il/elle/on est*	he/she/one is	*ils/elles sont*	they are

être is the verb people use most. This in fact explains why it is strange. Just as in English, the verb 'to be' has become distorted through being used so much!

Note that we have not given all the various meanings. For example ***je suis*** means both 'I am' and 'I am being', but we won't keep on telling you this again and again.

Practice 5.3

2. avoir

avoir **= to have**

	Singular		Plural	
1st person	*j'ai*	I have	*nous avons*	we have
2nd person	*tu as*	you have	*vous avez*	you have
3rd person	*il/elle/on a*	he/she/one has	*ils/elles ont*	they have

☠ Take care when saying *ils_ont, elles_ont*, so that they are not mistaken for *ils sont, elles sont*.

3. aller

aller **= to go**

	Singular		Plural	
1st person	*je vais*	I go	*nous allons*	we go
2nd person	*tu vas*	you go	*vous allez*	you go
3rd person	*il/elle/on va*	he/she/one goes	*ils/elles vont*	they go

☺ These two verbs are easy to learn together. Notice how similar their endings are, and how their *nous* and *vous* forms are predictable.

Two interesting points about avoir

1. Whereas in English we say 'there is' or 'there are', the phrase *il y a* is used for either in French. Literally it means: 'it has there' and is what is called an **impersonal** phrase.

   Example:
   Il y a trois couleurs dans le drapeau français.
   There are three colours in the French flag.

2. In French, a person **has** an age, rather than **being** so many years old; he **has** hot or cold, right or wrong, rather than **being** so; and he **has** fear, hunger or thirst, rather than **being** afraid, hungry or thirsty.

   Examples:

Mon grand-père a 100 ans.	My grandfather **is** 100 (**years old**).
*Nous **avons froid**, mais tu **as chaud**!*	We **are cold**, but you **are hot**!
*Vous **avez tort** et j'**ai raison**.*	You **are wrong** and I **am right**.
*Il **a peur** des chiens.*	He **is afraid/scared** of dogs.
*Tu **as faim**, ou **soif**?*	**Are** you **hungry**, or **thirsty**?

Practice 5.4 and 5.5

 CD 17

4. faire

faire = to do / to make / to do (an activity)

	Singular		Plural	
1st person	*je fais*	I do	*nous faisons*	we do
2nd person	*tu fais*	you do	*vous faites*	you do
3rd person	*il/elle/on fait*	he/she/one does	*ils/elles font*	they do

CD 18

5. prendre

prendre = to take

	Singular		Plural	
1st person	*je prends*	I take	*nous prenons*	we take
2nd person	*tu prends*	you take	*vous prenez*	you take
3rd person	*il/elle/on prend*	he/she/one takes	*ils/elles prennent*	they take

☺ Again, these two verbs are easy to learn together. Notice how they are quite similar to *–er* verbs.

Practice 5.6 to 5.8

To find out more about irregular verbs, see Chapter 19, pages 53-56.

The imperative

The *tu, nous* and *vous* forms of the present tense can also be used to give orders, without using the words *tu, nous* and *vous*. This is called the **imperative**.

Examples:
Regarde cette drôle de voiture!
Look at this funny car! (familiar singular)

Faisons un pique-nique!
Let's have a picnic!

Allez vite au guichet des renseignements!
Go to the information desk quickly! (familiar plural / formal)

From this you can see that the imperative may be 2nd person singular (when you are giving an order to one person you can be familiar with - 'Do it!'); 1st person plural (when you are giving an order to yourself and others - 'Let's do it!') or 2nd person plural (when you are giving an order to more than one person or are being formal/polite - 'Do it!').

Forming these imperatives from regular verbs is easy. They are the same as the present tense verb forms, with one small difference: in the 2nd person singular imperative, if the last vowel is an '**e**', which it normally is, the '**s**' is left off the end.

e.g.   *tu regard**es*** = 'you look'; ***regarde!*** = 'look!'
        nous regardons = 'we look'; ***regardons!*** = 'let's look!'
        vous regardez = 'you (pl.) look'; ***regardez!*** = 'look!'

Practice 5.9

Chapter 6: The future tense

CD 20

'I'm going to ...'

☺ It is really easy to express things in the future.
As in English, all you have to do is to say you **are going to do** (or **be**) them.

> Et qu'est-ce que tu **vas être** plus tard?

> Je **vais être** plus grand!

'And what are you **going to** be later?'

'I am **going to be** bigger!'

Remember the verb *aller*?

aller = to go

	Singular		**Plural**	
1st person	*je vais*	I am going	*nous allons*	we are going
2nd person	*tu vas*	you are going	*vous allez*	you are going
3rd person	*il/elle/on va*	he/she/one is going	*ils/elles vont*	they are going

Simply use *aller* followed by the infinitive (dictionary form) of the verb that shows what you are **going to do** (or **be**).

Examples:

*Je **vais aller** au restaurant.*	I'm **going to go** to the restaurant.
*Ma copine **va venir** avec moi.*	My girlfriend is **going to come** with me.
*Nous **allons manger** des frites.*	We are **going to eat** chips.
*Puis ses cousins **vont arriver**.*	Then her cousins are **going to arrive**.
*Après, nous **allons voir** un film.*	Afterwards, we are **going to see** a film.

To find out more about the future tense, see Chapter 20, page 57.

Practice 6.1 and 6.2

Chapter 7: | Accents

Be 'acute': avoid 'grave' mistakes!

Accents are the small squiggly signs that you sometimes see above a vowel. Many languages have accents and other signs, although English does not.

☺ Accents can be helpful.

There are three different sorts of accent:

'I just add an accent here and there, to make it look pretty!'

1. The acute accent – l'accent aigu: ╱

Used only on the letter '**e**', the acute accent changes the sound of the '**e**': '**é**' has the same sound as '**-ez**' and '**-er**' (set your mouth in a half-hearted smile as you say it).

Examples:

l'*été*	summer
j'ai regardé	I watched
le Sénégal	Senegal
la télé	the TV
vous regardez	you watch
regarder	to watch

☺ This accent is very useful to help you recognise the past tense. (See Chapter 8, page 19.)

Many French people regularly spell wrongly words ending in '-**er**', '-**é**' or '-**ez**'. Many English speaking people don't know the difference between 'it's' and 'its', 'their' and 'there' – it is the same type of mistake!

Practice 7.1

2. The grave accent – l'accent grave: ╲

When it is on the letter '**e**', the grave accent changes the sound of the '**e**': '**è**' has the same sound as '**ai**', '**et**', and '**e**' followed by two consonants (open your mouth a bit more as you say it).

Examples:

ma *mère*	my mother
j'*ai*	I have
un paqu*et*	a packet
elle *est*	she is

Note: To make them easier to say, some verbs have a change of sound with the *je, tu, il, elle, on, ils, elles* forms, shown by a grave accent (as in: **acheter** = to buy, **répéter** = to repeat) or a doubling of the consonant (as in: **appeler** = to call, **jeter** = to throw away).

♟ Although it is easy to hear the sound change, you cannot guess whether it will be spelt '**è**' or '**e**' + two consonants. A dictionary will tell you.

Examples:
è: acheter ⇒ j'ach**è**te, tu ach**è**tes, il/elle/on ach**è**te, nous achetons, vous achetez, ils/elles ach**è**tent.
e + double consonant: appeler ⇒ j'app**ell**e, tu app**ell**es, il/elle/on app**ell**e, nous appelons, vous appelez, ils/elles app**ell**ent.

When the accent is on the letters '**a**' and '**u**', it does not change their sound.
☺ But a grave accent on **à** and **ù** is very useful to help you tell two similar-looking words apart.

Examples:
là / la there / the
où / ou where / or

Practice 7.2

3. The circumflex – l'accent circonflexe: ∧

When it is on the letter '**e**', it changes its sound: '**ê**' has the same sound as '**è**'.
When it is on the letters '**a**', '**i**', '**o**', '**u**', it does not change their sound.
You may have seen it on phrases used in English such as 'village **fête**' and '**tête à tête**'.

☺ This accent shows a missing letter – usually '**s**'. This often helps you guess the meaning of a word, but not always!

Examples:
*le ch**â**teau* the castle
*une **î**le* an isle / island
*l'h**ô**pital* the hospital
*la fen**ê**tre* the window

☺ It can also help you tell two similar-looking words apart.

Examples:
tache stain   *t**â**che* task
sur on   *s**û**r* sure, safe
du some / of the   *d**û*** had to
mur wall   *m**û**r* ripe / mature
jeune young   *je**û**ne* fasting

To find out more about signs on letters, see Chapter 13, page 32.

Practice 7.3 to 7.5

Chapter 8: The past tense

'I've done it!'

When you were very young, you probably said things like: 'I eated', 'I gived', 'I drinked', 'I readed', 'I writed'. If you did, you were making irregular verbs behave like regular ones. Many common French verbs are irregular, too.

The perfect tense of –er verbs

☺ Remember the 4000 regular **–er** verbs in the present tense? Nearly all of them are regular in the past as well.

The main past tense in French is called the **perfect tense**. 'Perfect' simply means that the action is 'completed'. This tense exists in English, but often the '**has**' or '**have**' are left out, giving a tense called the simple past.

To form the perfect tense in French, start with a part of **avoir** (e.g. 'I have', 'you have' etc.) and follow this with the action done (e.g. 'bought', 'listened' etc.), changing the '**–er**' of the verb's infinitive to '**–é**'.

> **Examples**:
> *J'ai acheté un nouveau CD.*   I (have) bought a new CD.
> *Mon copain a téléphoné.*   My friend (has) 'phoned.
> *Il m'a invité.*   He (has) invited me.
> *Nous avons écouté le CD.*   We (have) listened to the CD.

In French the perfect tense is called the *passé composé* (compound past). This is because the verb is composed of two words.

Let's look at the verb **jouer** (to play) in the *passé composé*:

jouer = to play

	Singular		**Plural**	
1st person	*j'ai joué*	I (**have**) play**ed**	*nous avons joué*	we (**have**) play**ed**
2nd person	*tu as joué*	you (**have**) play**ed**	*vous avez joué*	you (**have**) play**ed**
3rd person	*il/elle/on a joué*	he/she/one (**has**) played	*ils/elles ont joué*	they (**have**) play**ed**

Practice 8.1

☺ **A few helpful hints!**

1. You **cannot leave out the** 'have' part in French, as often happens in English. (It is called the **auxiliary**, meaning 'helper'.)

2. The action you have done uses a special form (called the **past participle**) with the ending '**–é**' instead of the '**–er**' of the infinitive. In English, this ending is often '**–ed**'.

3. We saw '**–é**' when we were talking about accents. Here it acts as a signal that the action is in the past. It is a strong sound, easy to recognise.

4. If you think of the French name, ***passé composé***, it reminds you of what to do: you need to add a word (part of **avoir**) and use the ending '**–é**'.

This works for about 90% of **–er** verbs, but you will notice some that do not follow this pattern exactly. (See Chapter 21, page 60.)

Practice 8.2

The past tense of irregular verbs

We know that some verbs are irregular, and it should not surprise us to find that these verbs are irregular in the perfect tense, too. Look at the examples below:

1. faire

faire = to do/to make/to do (an activity)

	Singular		Plural	
1st person	*j'ai fait*	I did	*nous avons fait*	we did
2nd person	*tu as fait*	you did	*vous avez fait*	you did
3rd person	*il/elle/on a fait*	he/she/one did	*ils/elles ont fait*	they did

2. prendre

prendre = to take

	Singular		Plural	
1st person	*j'ai pris*	I took	*nous avons pris*	we took
2nd person	*tu as pris*	you took	*vous avez pris*	you took
3rd person	*il/elle/on a pris*	he/she/one took	*ils/elles ont pris*	they took

As you can see, the only strange thing is that they don't have the ending '**–é**'. The same kind of thing happens to these verbs in English (do**ne**, ma**de**, tak**en**), and to many others (eat**en**, giv**en**, go**ne**, read). They have a different ending from the normal '**–ed**' and these forms just have to be learnt.

Practice 8.3

The perfect tense with être

☃ Some verbs form their perfect tense using **être** as the auxiliary rather than **avoir**.

---

aller = to go

		Singular			Plural	
1st person		*je **suis** allé(e)*	I went		*nous **sommes** allé(e)s*	we went
2nd person		*tu **es** allé(e)*	you went		*vous **êtes** allé(e)s*	you went
3rd person		*il/elle/on **est** allé(e)*	he/she/one went		*ils/elles **sont** allé(e)s*	they went

---

It is really like saying: '**I am** gone', '**you are** gone', '**he is** gone', etc. Notice how the past participle has to 'agree' with the subject of the verb. If the subject is feminine we add '**e**', if plural we add '**s**' and if feminine **and** plural we add '**es**'.

To find out more about the perfect tense with *être*, see Chapter 22, page 62.

 Practice 8.4

The imperfect tense

☃ Even stranger: **être** and **avoir** are rarely found in the perfect tense. When used in the past, they are mostly in another tense called the **imperfect** (this means 'not completed'). This is what they look like:

être = to be

	Singular			Plural	
1st person	*j'étais*	I was		*nous étions*	we were
2nd person	*tu étais*	you were		*vous étiez*	you were
3rd person	*il/elle/on était*	he/she/one was		*ils/elles étaient*	they were

---

avoir = to have

	Singular			Plural	
1st person	*j'avais*	I had		*nous avions*	we had
2nd person	*tu avais*	you had		*vous aviez*	you had
3rd person	*il/elle/on avait*	he/she/one had		*ils/elles avaient*	they had

---

☺ Remember, 90% of French verbs are easy to learn. And you learnt the past tense in English – which is really difficult!

To find out more about the imperfect tense, see Chapter 23, page 65.

Practice 8.5 to 8.8

Chapter 9: | Question Time

CD 28

Who? Where? When? How?
What? How many? Why?
How long? How much? Which?

'Qui est-ce que je suis? Où est-ce que je suis? Quand est-ce que je suis arrivé ici? Comment est-ce que je suis arrivé ici? Qu'est-ce que je fais ici? Combien de fois est-ce que je suis déjà venu ici? Pourquoi est-ce que je suis ici? Combien de temps est-ce que je vais rester ici? Combien coûte ce chien dans la vitrine? Quel chien?'

'**Who** am I? **Where** am I? **When** did I get here? **How** did I get here? **What** am I doing here? **How many** times have I been here before?
Why am I here? **How long** am I going to stay here? **How much** is that doggy in the window? **Which** dog?'

Questions are not easy to form in English. In most cases you need to add 'do', 'does' or 'did', but sometimes you turn the sentence round.

Examples:

Statement	Question
Mike had his walkman.	**Did** Mike **have** his walkman? (Add 'did', change 'had' to 'have').
He has bought a CD player.	**Has he** bought a CD player? (Change round)
He is at home.	**Is he** at home? (change round).
He listens to his music all day.	**Does** he **listen** to his music all day? (Add 'does', change 'listens' to 'listen')
His parents want him to stop.	**Do** his parents want him to stop? (Add 'do')

Questions in French

There are several ways of turning statements into questions in French.

☺ One way is very easy: simply put the phrase ***est-ce que*** (meaning 'is it [true] that') in front of the statement, put a question mark at the end, and raise your voice enquiringly!

Note: the ***que*** shortens to ***qu'*** before a vowel sound.

Examples:

Statement	**Question**
Mike avait son baladeur.	***Est-ce que*** *Mike avait son baladeur?*
Il a acheté un lecteur de CD.	***Est-ce qu'****il a acheté un lecteur de CD?*
Il est chez lui maintenant.	***Est-ce qu'****il est chez lui maintenant?*
Il écoute sa musique toute la journée.	***Est-ce qu'****il écoute sa musique toute la journée?*
Ses parents veulent qu'il s'arrête.	***Est-ce que*** *ses parents veulent qu'il s'arrête?*

Practice 9.1

Questions with precise question words

If you need to ask a more precise question, with a question word like 'why', 'how', etc., you still follow the same pattern.

Examples:

Where did you buy your jumper?	***Où*** *est-ce que tu as acheté ton pull?*
When was it?	***Quand*** *est-ce que c'était?*
How did you pay?	***Comment*** *est-ce que tu as payé?*
What are you going to wear with it?	***Qu'****est-ce que tu vas mettre avec?*
Which colour do you prefer?	***Quelle***** couleur est-ce que tu préfères?*
How many black jumpers do you have?	***Combien*** *est-ce que tu as de pulls noirs?*
Why did you buy a black one?	***Pourquoi*** *est-ce que tu en as acheté un noir?*
Who are you going to the party with?	*Avec **qui** est-ce que tu vas à la fête?*
How long are you going to stay?	***Combien de temps*** *est-ce que tu vas rester?*

*To find out more about the different endings of **quel**, see Chapter 15, page 42, and for questions generally, see Chapter 24, page 67.

see Chapter 15, page 42, and for questions generally, see Chapter 24, page 67.

Practice 9.2

Combien de temps est-ce que tu vas rester?

'How long are you going to stay?'

Chapter 10: | Negatives

It's not a problem!

Negatives are far from easy to form in English. In most cases you need to add 'don't', 'doesn't', or 'didn't', but sometimes you just add 'not' or its short form '–n't'.

Examples:

Positive	**Negative**
Mike had his walkman.	Mike didn't have his walkman. (Add 'didn't', change 'had' to 'have')
He has bought a CD player.	He has not bought a CD player. (Just add 'not').
He is at home now.	He isn't at home now. (Add '–n't')
He listens to his music all day.	He doesn't listen to his music all day. (Add 'doesn't', change 'listens' to 'listen')
His parents want him to stop.	His parents don't want him to stop. (Add 'don't')

Negatives in French

☺ By contrast, it is very easy to make a French sentence negative: simply put the words **ne** and **pas** around the verb. Note: the **ne** shortens to **n'** before a vowel sound.

Examples:

Positive	**Negative**
Mike avait son baladeur.	*Mike **n'**avait **pas** son baladeur.*
Il a acheté un lecteur de CD.	*Il **n'a pas** acheté un lecteur de CD.*
Il est chez lui maintenant.	*Il **n'est pas** chez lui maintenant.*
Il écoute sa musique toute la journée.	*Il **n'écoute pas** sa musique toute la journée.*
Ses parents veulent qu'il s'arrête.	*Ses parents **ne** veulent **pas** qu'il s'arrête.*

Practice 10.1

Negatives in the perfect tense

Did you notice the sentence in the perfect tense? The two negative words go round the ***avoir*** part and the past participle comes after, as happens in English.

Examples:

*Je **n'**invite **pas** d'adultes à ma fête.*	I'm not inviting any adults to my party.	Present
*Je **n'ai pas** invité d'adultes à ma fête.*	I have not invited any adults to my party.	Past
*Mon copain **ne** téléphone **pas**.*	My friend is not telephoning.	Present
*Mon copain **n'a pas** téléphoné.*	My friend did not telephone.	Past
*Mous **n'écoutons pas** la musique.*	We aren't listening to the music.	Present
*Nous **n'avons pas** écouté la musique.*	We didn't listen to the music.	Past

To find out more about negatives, see Chapter 25, page 71.

Practice 10.2

Chapter 11: Prepositions

From me to you!

> Où est-ce que j'ai laissé mes devoirs en rentrant **du** cinéma? **Sur** la table, **sous** le lit, **derrière** l'armoire? Non, **dans** le chien! Comment est-ce que je peux le donner **au** professeur maintenant?

'Where did I leave my homework after I came back **from** the cinema? **On** the table, **under** the bed, **behind** the wardrobe? No, **in** the dog! How can I give it **to** the teacher now?'

Remember? A **preposition** comes before a noun (or pronoun), to introduce it.

Generally, prepositions are quite easy to use in French. However, there are two which need to be handled with care.

à

Usually *à* is the equivalent of '**at**' or '**to**' in English.

Examples:	
Eric est allé à Londres.	Eric went **to** London.
Je donne des chocolats à ma mère.	I give some chocolates **to** my mother.
Ma sœur arrive à huit heures	My sister is arriving **at** eight o'clock.

When you need to say 'at the' or 'to the', this is what happens:

Feminine singular:	à + la	→	*no problem*	*à la piscine*	'at/to the swimming pool'
Vowel sound singular:	à + l'	→	*no problem*	*à l'hôtel*	'at/to the hotel'
Masculine singular:	à + le	→	***careful!*** ☠	***au** club*	'at/to the club'
All plurals:	à + les	→	***careful!*** ☠	***aux** magasins*	'at/to the shops'

This makes it easier to say.

Examples:	
Eric est allé à la piscine.	Eric went to the (swimming) pool.
Ben est allé à l'exposition.	Ben went to the exhibition.
J'ai offert des chocolats au voisin.	I offered some chocolates to the neighbour.
Ma sœur donne du sucre aux_éléphants.	My sister gives some sugar to the elephants.

à with towns and countries

Where in English, 'in' or 'to' is used before towns and countries, in French, **à** is used before towns, **au** (**à** + **le**) with masculine countries, and **aux** (**à** + **les**) with plural countries.

Examples:
*Céline habite **à** Montréal **au** Canada.*   Céline lives **in** Montreal **in** Canada.
*Elle va **à** New York **aux** Etats-Unis.*   She goes **to** New York **in** the United States.

However, with feminine countries (the majority), **en** is used.

Examples:
*Edith habitait **à** Paris **en** France.*   Edith used to live **in** Paris **in** France.
*Elle allait souvent **en** Italie.*   She often used to go **to** Italy.

Practice 11.1

de

Usually **de** is the equivalent of 'of' or 'from' in English.

Examples:
*Eric vient **de** Bruxelles.*   Eric comes **from** Brussels.
*Ben vient **d'**Amiens.*   Ben comes **from** Amiens.
*Je parle **de** mon père.*   I'm talking **about** (**of**) my father.

When you need to say 'of the' or 'from the', this is what happens:

Feminine singular:	*de + la*	→ *no problem*	**de la** *piscine*	'of/from the pool'
Vowel sound singular:	*de + l'*	→ *no problem*	**de l'**hôtel	'of/from the hotel'
Masculine singular:	*de + le*	→ **careful!** ☠	**du** *club*	'of/from the club'
All plurals:	*de + les*	→ **careful!** ☠	**des** *magasins*	'of/from the shops'

This makes it easier to say.

Examples:
*Eric vient **de la** campagne.*   Eric comes **from the** country(side).
*Ben vient **de l'**exposition.*   Ben is coming **from the** exhibition.
*Je parle **du** stade où je vais.*   I'm talking **about** (**of**) **the** stadium where I go.
*Nous rentrons **des** Etats-Unis.*   We are returning **from the** United States.

Note: this also happens when **de** is part of a phrase, like **beaucoup de**, or **à côté de**.

Examples:
*Ma sœur a **beaucoup d'**amis.*   My sister has **a lot of** friends.
***Beaucoup des** joueurs sont français.*   **A lot of the** players are French.
*Elle habite **à côté de** Calais.*   She lives **next to** (literally: **by the side of**) Calais.
*Elle habite **à côté de la** gare.*   She lives **next to the** station (literally: **by the side of the**) station.

Practice 11.2

de, d', du, de la, de l', des (showing possession)

In French we cannot use the '**apostrophe s**' to show possession, as is done in English. Instead we say 'of' or 'of the'.

Examples:

*Voici le père **de** Frédéric.*	This is Frédéric**'s** father. (literally: the father **of** …)
*C'est le chien **du** voisin.*	It's the neighbour**'s** dog. (literally: the dog **of the** …)
*Où est la plume **de la** tante?*	Where is the aunt**'s** pen? (literally: the pen **of the** …)
*La mère **de l'**enfant est française.*	The child**'s** mother is French. (literally: the mother **of the** …)
*Elle n'a pas l'adresse **des** voisins.*	She does not have the neighbour**s'** address. (literally: the address **of the** …)

 Practice 11.3

du, de la, de l', des (meaning 'some')

The words *du, de la, de l', des* are also used to mean 'some'. It is like saying: '(some) of the'. In English, the word 'some' is often left out. We cannot do that in French.

Examples:

*Au restaurant, je mange **de la** viande.*	At the restaurant I eat (**some**) meat.
*Avec, je commande **des** frites.*	With it I order (**some**) chips.
*Puis je prends **du** gâteau.*	Then I have (**some**) cake.
*Quelquefois je bois **de l'**eau.*	Sometimes I drink (**some**) water.

Practice 11.4

Note: If the sentence is negative, *de la, de l', du, des* all become *de,* (*d'* before a vowel sound). In English you have to change the 'some' to 'any', and it is often left out.

Examples:

*Les végétariens **ne** mangent **pas de** viande.*	Vegetarians don't eat (**any**) meat.
*Quoi! Tu **ne** commandes **pas de** frites?*	What! You're not ordering (**any**) chips?
*La grosse dame **ne** prend **pas de** gâteau.*	The fat lady does not have (**any**) cake.
*Le petit bébé **ne** boit **pas d'**eau.*	The little baby does not drink (**any**) water.

Practice 11.5

Je n'ai pas d'argent!

Other prepositions

Usually the other French prepositions are straightforward. Here is a story using examples of some common ones:

Examples:

*Mathilde part juste **après** sept heures.*	Mathilde leaves just **after** seven.
*Elle va **chez** ses parents.*	She goes **to** her parents' **home**.
*Elle fait le trajet **en**[1] voiture.*	She travels **by** car.
*Elle arrive **avant** huit heures.*	She arrives **before** eight.
*Elle laisse sa voiture **derrière** le bâtiment.*	She leaves her car **behind** the building.
*Elle monte **à** l'appartement.*	She goes up **to** the flat.
*Elle apporte une boîte **de** chocolats.*	She brings a box **of** chocolates.
*Elle met les chocolats **sur** la table.*	She puts the chocolates **on** the table.
***Dans** le salon, elle discute **avec** son père.*	**In** the lounge, she chats **with** her father.
*Elle prépare un café **sans** sucre **pour** sa mère.*	She makes a coffee **without** sugar **for** her mother.
*Elle passe un moment **devant** la télé.*	She spends a while **in front of** the telly.
*Elle reste **pendant**[2] environ une heure, **jusqu'à** neuf heures.*	She stays **for** about one hour, **until** nine.
*Puis, elle va **en** ville.*	Then she goes **to** town.
*Il pleut, alors elle reste **sous** son parapluie.*	It is raining, so she stays **under** her umbrella.
*Puis elle rentre **entre** neuf heures et demie et dix heures.*	Then she returns **between** nine thirty and ten.

Notes:
1. If you are **inside** the vehicle, use *en* (*en train, en avion, en bus*). If you are **riding** the vehicle, use *à* (*à vélo, à cheval*, even *à pied*!).
2. See how to express 'for' below.

Practice 11.6

How to express 'for'

In most cases, the French equivalent of 'for' is *pour*.

Examples:

*Voici un cadeau **pour** toi.*	Here is a present **for** you.
*Nous prenons le train **pour** Londres.*	We are taking the train **for** London.

However, with expressions of time, we also use *depuis* or *pendant*. Look at the following examples:

Examples:

*J'habite en Ecosse **depuis**[1] un an.*	I have been living in Scotland **for** a year.
*J'ai voyagé en Europe **pendant**[2] deux mois.*	I travelled in Europe **for** two months.
*L'été prochain, je vais partir au Canada **pour**[3] trois semaines.*	Next summer, I'm going to go to Canada **for** three weeks.

Notes:
1. The action started in the past and is still going on now: 'for' = 'since'. The verb is in the present in French, but in the past in English.
2. The action started and finished in the past: 'for' = 'during'.
3. The action will take place in the future.

Practice 11.7

Chapter 12: Pronouns

 ## French grammar? It's easy!

A **pronoun** replaces a noun to avoid repeating it. Of course you must not overdo pronouns, or your message will not be clear.

Subject pronouns

You have already used pronouns when you were learning verbs: *je/j'*, *tu*, *il*, *elle*, *on*, *nous*, *vous*, *ils*, *elles*. They save repeating the names of people or things.

The noun or pronoun referring to the person or thing doing the action of the verb is called the **subject**.

Examples:	
Jack arrive de Londres.	**Jack** is arriving from London.
Il arrive de Londres.	**He** is arriving from London.
Brigitte et sa sœur habitent à Amiens.	**Brigitte and her sister** live in Amiens.
Elles habitent à Amiens.	**They** live in Amiens.
Le lapin est dans sa cage.	**The rabbit** is in its cage.
Il est dans sa cage.	**It** is in its cage.
Mes sœurs ont beaucoup d'amis.	**My sisters** have a lot of friends.
Elles ont beaucoup d'amis.	**They** have a lot of friends.

Practice 12.1

Object pronouns

The noun or pronoun showing to whom or what the action is happening, is called the **object**. Just as the subject of a verb can be replaced by a subject pronoun, the object can be replaced by an object pronoun.

Examples:	
*Je connais **Eric**.*	I know **Eric**.
*Je **le** connais.*	I know **him**.
*Il aime **Brigitte**.*	He likes **Brigitte**.
*Il **l'**aime.*	He likes **her**.
*Nous invitons **Eric et Brigitte** au cinéma.*	We are inviting **Eric and Brigitte** to the cinema.
*Nous **les** invitons au cinéma.*	We are inviting **them** to the cinema.
*Nous **t'**invitons aussi.*	We invite **you** as well.
*Viens, s'il **te** plaît.*	Do come please (if it pleases **you**).

As you can see, the **subject** is in charge of the verb, and the **object** is the person or thing on the receiving end of the verb.

Subject pronouns		Object pronouns	
I	*je / j'* (+ vowel)	me	*me / m'* (+ vowel)
you (familiar singular)	*tu*	you (familiar singular)	*te / t'* (+ vowel)
he	*il*	him	*le / l'* (+ vowel)
she	*elle*	her	*la / l'* (+ vowel)
it	*il* (m.) / *elle* (f.)	it	*le* (m.) / *la* (f.) / *l'* (+ vowel)
we	*nous*	us	*nous*
you (formal / plural)	*vous*	you (formal / plural)	*vous*
they	*ils* (m.) / *elles* (f.)	them	*les*

☠ In French, the object pronoun does not go in the same place as it does in English. It is positioned just before the verb.

Examples:

*Nicole **nous** appelle.*	Nicole calls **us**.
*Nous **la** voyons.*	We (can) see **her**.
Elle présente son voisin.	She introduces her neighbour.
*Nous **les** emmenons au cinéma.*	We take **them** to the cinema.
*Ils **m'**accompagnent au guichet.*	They accompany **me** to the ticket office.
Nous achetons quatre billets.	We buy four tickets.
*Nicole **les** paye.*	Nicole pays for **them**.
*Nous **la** remercions.*	We thank **her**.

Practice 12.2 to 12.4

Congratulations! You've got to grips with the **Bare Bones** of French. Now, in Part Two, you can build on your achievement with **Body Building**.

Part Two: Body Building

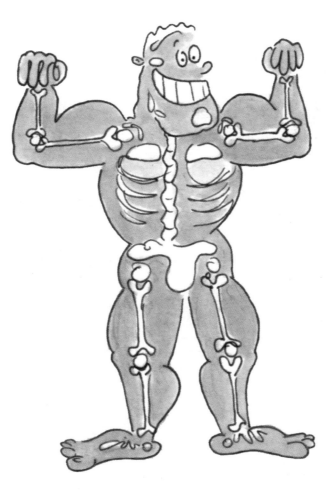

Chapter 13: | More squiggles!

The 'fish hook' and the 'two funny dots': what are they for?

Remember? **Accents** (Chapter 7, page 17) are a signal above a letter; they either change the pronunciation or provide a helpful detail about a word.

Other signs sometimes placed under or above letters are a thing that looks like a fish hook under the letter '*c*' (the **cedilla**), and two funny dots, side by side, over vowels (the **tréma**).

Cher Père Noël, cette année, je voudrais un beau garçon musclé, et même …

'Dear Father Christmas, this year I would like a gorgeous muscular boy, and even …'

The cedilla

A **cedilla**, which may only be added under the letter '*c*', changes the sound of the '*c*' from '*k*' to '*s*'. Normally, the letter '*c*' is pronounced as 's' in front of '*e*', '*i*', '*y*' (the same sort of thing happens in English too: century, cinema, bicycle); but as '*k*' before '*a*', '*o*', '*u*' (as in English: car, coronation, custard).

To produce the sound '*s*' in front of '*a*', '*o*', '*u*', we put a cedilla under the '*c*'.

Examples:
'*s*' sound:

cela	this
un principe	a principle
un cygne	a swan
la façade	the front (e.g. of a building)
un garçon	a boy
un reçu	a receipt
'*k*' sound:	
un cadeau	a gift
un correspondant	a penpal
la cuisine	the kitchen

Note: A cedilla is used with the **nous** form, in the present tense, of verbs ending in '-**cer**' (such as **lancer** = to throw, **commencer** = to begin, **menacer** = to threaten) to keep the '**s**' sound in front of '**o**'.

> **Example:**
> **'s'** sound:
> *je lance, tu lances, il lance, nous lan**ç**ons, vous lancez, ils lancent.*

A similar thing happens with verbs ending in '-**ger**' (such as **manger** = to eat, **ranger** = to tidy), but obviously not with a cedilla. To keep a soft sound in the **nous** form, an '**e**' is added after the '**g**' (otherwise the sound would be hard, as in the English word 'mango').

> **Example:**
> soft '**g**' sound:
> *je mange, tu manges, il mange, nous mang**e**ons, vous mangez, ils mangent.*

Practice 13.1

The tréma

The **tréma**, which appears only on a vowel, tells you to pronounce that vowel separately from the vowel next to it.

Examples:

aigu (m), *aiguë* (f)	sharp
contrast with:	
bague	ring (on finger)
vague	wave (on sea)
catalogue	catalogue
Noël	Christmas
contrast with:	
moelle	marrow
naïf	naïve
contrast with:	
maison	house
naissance	birth

Je peux couper **Joëlle** en deux avec ma formule magique!

'I can chop **Joëlle** in two with my magic trick!'

Aïe!

Sometimes the same effect is produced by using '**h**' or '**y**' in the middle of a word.

Examples:

un cahier	an exercise book
le loyer	the rent

Note that accents, cedillas and trémas are not normally used with capital letters.

Practice 13.2 and 13.3

Chapter 14: Masculine or feminine?

CD
42

More tips about the gender of nouns

Remember? All French **nouns** are either masculine or feminine (see Chapter 2, page 4).

☺ The following tips will help you to know whether a noun is masculine or feminine.

> Nous voici au ci**rque**, avec M. Macho, sur le petit é**cran**. Etant psycho**logue**, il sait qu'il prend un ris**que** sur le câ**ble**, avec un chapeau mais pas de cas**que**, et sans para**chute**. Quel optim**isme**!

'Here we are at the circus, with Mr Macho, on the TV screen. Being a psychologist, he knows he is taking a risk on the cable, with a hat but no helmet and without a parachute. What optimism!'

Masculine endings

A noun is likely to be **masculine** if:

(i) it has a **consonant as the last letter** (except '–*ion*' ending):

Examples:

estomac	stomach
amour	love
tennis	tennis
assistant	assistant
boucher	butcher
acteur	actor
Sénégal	Senegal

But watch out! *sœur* (sister) is feminine, obviously!

(ii) it ends in '–*i*' or '–*u*':

Examples:

ami	friend
souci	concern
jeu	game
genou	knee
chapeau	hat

(iii) it ends in '**–be**' or '**–ble**':

Examples:
sable	sand
câble	cable
tube	tube / hit song

But watch out! *table* (table) is feminine.

(iv) it ends with '**–ège**':

Examples:
collège	secondary school
manège	riding school/fairground roundabout

(v) it ends in '**–isme**' or '**–iste**':

Examples:
optimisme	optimism
socialisme	socialism
artiste	artist
pianiste	pianist

(vi) it ends in '**–logue**':

Examples:
psychologue	psychologist
archéologue	archeologist
catalogue	catalogue

(vii) it ends with a **consonant** + '**–re**' or '**–que**':

Examples:
cadre	frame / executive
chiffre	digit / figure
casque	helmet
risque	risk

But watch out! *chambre* (bedroom) is feminine.

(viii) it begins with '**porte-**' or '**para**-':

Examples:
portefeuille	wallet
porte-clés	key-ring
parapluie	umbrella
parachute	parachute

Practice 14.1

Feminine endings

A noun is likely to be **feminine** if:

(i) it ends in '**–on**' (even more likely to be feminine if it ends in '**–ion**', often the same or a similar word in English):

> **Examples:**
> *leçon*   lesson
> *raison*   reason / right
> **But watch out!** *garçon* (boy), *crayon* (pencil), and a few more are masculine.
>
> *télévision*   television
> *compétition*   competition
> But watch out! *avion* (plane) is masculine (many French people think it is feminine!).

(ii) it ends in '**–té**' (often similar word ending with **–ty** in English) or '**–tié**':

> **Examples:**
> *liberté*   liberty / freedom
> *égalité*   equality
> *fraternité*   fraternity
> *pitié*   pity
> *amitié*   friendship
>
> But watch out! *comité* (committee) is masculine.

(iii) it ends in '**–ie**' , '**–ue**' , or '**–ée**':

> **Examples:**
> *bougie*   candle
> *maladie*   illness
> *rue*   street
> *avenue*   avenue
> *cheminée*   chimney
> *bouchée*   mouthful
>
> But watch out! *musée* (museum) and *lycée* (6th form college) are masculine.

(iv) it ends in '**–ance**', '**–anse**', or '**–ence**' (all have the same sound, often the same or similar word in English):

> **Examples:**
> *chance*   chance
> *danse*   dance
> *patience*   patience
>
> But watch out! *silence* (silence) is masculine.

(v) it ends in '**–se**', '**–rice**', or '**–ère**' (often the feminine version of a masculine noun ending in '**–eur**' or '**–er**'):

Examples:

chanteuse	female singer
entorse	sprain
directrice	female director / headmistress
institutrice	female primary school teacher
infirmière	female nurse
bière	beer

But watch out! *père* (father), and *frère* (brother) are masculine (of course!).

(vi) it ends in '**–(t)te**' (but not '**–iste**'), or '**–(n)ne**' (often the feminine version of a masculine noun ending in '**–t**' or '**–n**'):

Examples:

chatte	female cat
assistante	female assistant
porte	door
chienne	female dog
mine	mine (e.g. gold or diamond)

But watch out! *reste* (remainder) is masculine.

(vii) it ends in '**–(l)le**' or '**–(p)pe**':

Examples:

ville	town
file	queue
nappe	tablecloth
pipe	pipe

But watch out! *groupe* (group) is masculine.

(viii) it ends in '**–che**':

Examples:

douche	shower (in bathroom)
fiche	form (card)
mouche	fly (insect)
ruche	beehive

But watch out! *dimanche* (Sunday) is masculine.

(ix) it ends with a **vowel** + '**–re**' or '**–que**':

Examples:

confiture	jam
paire	pair
clinique	clinic

Practice 14.2

Nous voici à la cli**nique**. Je suis son assist**ante**. Cette compéti**tion** à la télévi**sion** va lui servir de le**çon**, j'espère. Par ami**tié**, je vais traiter l'ent**orse** et l'aider pendant sa malad**ie**.

'Here we are at the clinic. I am his (female) assistant. This competition on television is going to teach him a lesson, I hope. Out of friendship, I shall treat the sprain and help him during his illness.'

Gender swap!

☠ A small number of nouns are sometimes masculine, sometimes feminine, with a different meaning.

Examples:

Masculine		**Feminine**	
un livre	a book	*une livre*	a pound (£/lb)
un voile	a veil	*une voile*	a sail
le vase	the vase	*la vase*	the sludge
un page	a page boy	*une page*	a page (of a book)
un mode	a mode/method	*une mode*	a fashion/style
le tour	the tour	*la tour*	the tower
un moule	a cake tin	*une moule*	a mussel
un somme	a nap	*une somme*	a sum
un mousse	a sailor boy	*une mousse*	mousse/froth/moss

Le mariage: le marié était **un mousse**, la mariée portait **un voile**. Il y avait deux petits **pages** et beaucoup de fleurs dans **un vase**...?

'The wedding: the bridegroom was a mousse, the bride was wearing a sail. There were two small pages, and a lot of flowers in a sludge...?'

As you can see, getting the gender wrong can be rather unfortunate!

The context also helps differentiate between them. This can also be the case in English. Think of the various meanings of the word fast: 'stuck fast', 'a fast car', 'going fast', 'they fast for Ramadan', 'the fast lasts for a month'.

Practice 14.3 and 14.4

Chapter 15: Adjectives

Before or after the noun?
More about agreements, and how to make comparisons

Remember? Most French **adjectives** go after their noun. They become masculine or feminine, singular or plural, to match their noun. This is normally done by adding '**–e**' for feminine, and '**–s**' for plural, on the end of the adjective (see Chapter 4, page 8).

Adjectives following their noun

Unlike English adjectives, which always go in front of their noun, **most** French adjectives, including those of colour, nationality and shape, **follow** their noun.

Examples:

un chanteur français	a French singer
une chemise verte	a green shirt
un ventre rond	a pot belly
une actrice célèbre	a famous actress
des moustaches noires	a black moustache

Practice 15.1

Adjectives preceding their noun

A small number of French adjectives, however, go **before** their noun: *autre, beau, bon, grand, gros, haut, jeune, joli, long, mauvais, nouveau, petit, vieux.*

Examples:

une autre fois	another time
un beau bateau	a beautiful boat
un bon hôtel	a good hotel
le grand monument	the tall monument
le gros repas	the big meal
la haute tour	the high tower
le jeune homme	the young man
la jolie fille	the pretty girl
le long trajet	the long journey
un mauvais jour	a bad day
un nouveau magazine	a new magazine
le petit garçon	the little boy
un vieux bateau	an old boat

Practice 15.2

Moi, j'aime la haute cuisine!

Note: Sometimes these adjectives **follow** the noun in order to add emphasis, often preceded by a word such as *vraiment, très* or *bien*.

Examples:
C'était un repas vraiment bon!	It was a really good meal!
Ils ont une maison très jolie.	They have a very nice house.

CD 45

♟ Just as a small number of nouns have a different meaning depending on whether they are masculine or feminine (see Chapter 14 page 38), a few French adjectives have a different meaning according to their position, e.g. *ancien, cher, pauvre, propre, seul.*

Examples:
un ancien collègue	a former colleague
un château ancien	an old castle
mon cher cousin	my dear cousin
mon ordinateur cher	my dear / expensive computer
le pauvre enfant!	the poor child!
un pays pauvre	a poor country
son propre père	his own father
un pull propre	a clean jumper
un seul jour	only one day / a single day
un homme seul	a man on his own

The adjectives *dernier* and *prochain* go **before** the noun, except with days, weeks, months and years, when they normally go after the noun.

Examples:
le dernier métro	the last underground train
le mois dernier	last month
la prochaine fois	next time
la semaine prochaine	next week

Practice 15.3 and 15.4

More about the agreement of adjectives

CD 46

Unlike English adjectives, **French adjectives add an ending**, to match the **gender** (masculine or feminine) and the **number** (singular or plural) of their noun (see Chapter 4, page 8).

The ending is '**–e**' for feminine, unless the masculine adjective already ends in '**–e**', in which case it does not change.

Examples:
un livre intéressant	an interesting book
une idée intéressante	an interesting idea
un livre moderne	a modern book
une idée moderne	a modern idea

The ending is '**–s**' for plural. If the singular adjective already ends in '**–s**', it does not change (the same as for nouns; see Chapter 2 page 5). This is also the case for adjectives ending in '**–x**'.

Examples:

un magazine intéressant	an interesting magazine
des** magazines intéressant**s	(some) interesting magazines
un magazine moderne	a modern magazine
des** magazines moderne**s	(some) modern magazines
*le gro**s** magazine*	the big magazine
***les** gro**s** magazines*	the big magazines
*un journal sérieu**x***	a serious newspaper
des** journaux sérieu**x	(some) serious newspapers

Note: The plural '**–s**' is silent, except if the next word starts with a vowel. Then it provides a useful linking sound.

'It's a low stocking.'
'No, it's a pair of low stockings!'

Examples:

un_anorak vert	*des_anoraks verts*
le petit_animal	*les petits_animaux*

 Practice 15.5

Irregular feminine adjectives

Some adjectives have irregular feminine singular forms.
Although they still add '**–e**', there are other changes that make them easier to say.

☺ Listen to them on the recording and repeat them – they will be easier to remember.

Adjectives which end in '**–f**' in the masculine end in '**–ve**' in the feminine.
(This is similar to 'dwar**f** – dwar**ve**s' in English).

Examples:

actif	→	*acti**ve***	active
neuf	→	*neu**ve***	new

Adjectives which end in '**–eau**' in the masculine end with '**–elle**' in the feminine.

Examples:

beau	→	*b**elle***	beautiful
nouveau	→	*nouv**elle***	new

Adjectives which end in '**–c**' in the masculine end with '**–che**' or '**–que**' in the feminine.

Examples:

blanc	→	*blan**che***	white
sec	→	*sè**che***	dry
similarly:			
public	→	*publi**que***	public

Adjectives which end in '*–er*' in the masculine end with '*–ère*' in the feminine.

Examples:
cher	→	*chère*	dear / expensive
dernier	→	*dernière*	last

Adjectives which end in '*–il*', '*-el*', '*-n*' or '*–s*' in the masculine usually double their last letter before adding '*–e*' in the feminine. (This is similar to 'fu**n** – fu**nn**y' in English).

Examples:
*genti**l***	→	*genti**lle***	kind
*nature**l***	→	*nature**lle***	natural
*que**l** ... ?*	→	*que**lle** ... ?*	which ...?
*ancie**n***	→	*ancie**nne***	former / old
*bo**n***	→	*bo**nne***	good
*ba**s***	→	*ba**sse***	low
*gro**s***	→	*gro**sse***	big / fat

Some, but not all, adjectives which end in '*–x*' in the masculine end with '*–se*' in the feminine (see below).

Examples:
*heureu**x***	→	*heureu**se***	happy
*sérieu**x***	→	*sérieu**se***	serious
but:			
*vieu**x***	→	*vie**ille***	old
*dou**x***	→	*dou**ce***	soft / mild
*fau**x***	→	*fau**sse***	wrong

The adjective *long* has the feminine *longue*.
The adjective *favori* has the feminine *favorite*.

☺ For the feminine plural, simply add '*–s*' to the feminine singular form.

Examples:
une revue intéressante	an interesting magazine
beaucoup de revues intéressantes	many interesting magazines
une chaussette blanche	a white sock
deux chaussettes blanches	two white socks
une personne active	an active person
des personnes actives	(some) active people

Practice 15.6

Strange masculine adjective forms

The adjectives **beau**, **nouveau** and **vieux** have developed alternative masculine singular forms – **bel**, **nouvel** and **vieil** – that make them easier to say in front of a vowel sound.
They have the same pronunciation as the feminine singular forms.

Examples:

un vieux château	an old castle
un vieil_homme	an old man
une vieille personne	an old person
le nouveau magasin	the new shop
le nouvel_an	the New Year
la nouvelle mode	the new / latest fashion
un beau vélo	a beautiful bike
un bel_avion	a beautiful plane
une belle voiture	a beautiful car

Practice 15.7

The comparative adjective

The comparative adjective is used to say that one thing or person is 'more ... than', 'less ... than', or 'as /so ... as' something or someone else:

plus ... que	more ... than / ...–er than
moins ... que	less ... than
aussi/si ... que	as / so ... as

'Je suis **plus** grand **que** toi.
Tu es **moins** intelligent **que** moi.
Tu n'es pas **aussi/si** fort **que** moi.'

Oui, mais je suis la créature **la plus** méchante et **la moins** agréable!'

The adjective still adds '**–e**' for feminine and '**–s**' for plural.

Examples:

*La place de concert est **plus** chère **que** la place de cinéma.*
The concert seat is dear**er than** the cinema seat.

*Les chanteurs anglais sont **plus** populaires **que** les chanteurs français.*
English singers are **more** popular **than** French singers.

*Les docteurs sont **moins** riches **que** les chanteurs pop.*
Doctors are **less** wealthy **than** pop singers.

*Et les profs sont encore **moins** riches!*
And teachers are even **less** wealthy!

*Certains joueurs de foot sont **aussi** célèbres **que** les chanteurs.*
Some footballers are **as** famous **as** singers.

Just as, in English, you say '**better** ... **than**' (and not 'gooder ... than'), in French, you say ***meilleur(e)(s)** ... **que**.*

Example:

*Le chocolat est bon, mais les légumes sont **meilleurs (que** le chocolat) à la santé!*

Chocolate is good, but vegetables are **better** (**than** chocolate) for your health!

The elephant to the mosquito:
'I am tall**er than** you. You are **less** intelligent **than** I am. You are not **as/so** strong **as** I am.'

The mosquito to the elephant:
'Yes but I am **the** nast**iest** and **the least** pleasant creature!'

Practice 15.8

CD
51

The superlative adjective

The superlative adjective is used to show that someone or something is 'very' or 'most' something.

> *le / la / les plus ...*   the most ... / the ...est
> *le / la / les moins ...* the least ...

The adjective still adds on '*–e*' for feminine and '*–s*' for plural.

> **Examples:**
> *Je ne veux pas acheter la place de théâtre **la plus chère**.*
> I don't want to buy **the** dear**est** theatre seat.
>
> *Les places **les plus chères** sont au balcon.*
> **The most** expensive seats are in the balcony.
>
> *On donne la pièce dans **le plus** vieux théâtre de Londres.*
> The play is showing in **the** old**est** theatre in London.
>
> *J'accepterai même la place **la moins confortable**!*
> I will accept even **the least comfortable** seat!

Just as, in English, you say 'the best' (and not 'the goodest'), in French, you say *le/la/les meilleur(e)(s)*.

> **Example:**
> ***La meilleure** sportive a **les meilleurs** résultats.*
> **The best** sportswoman has **the best** results.

Practice 15.9

Chapter 16: | More adjectives

Demonstrative and possessive adjectives: **this** book is **my** property!

> **Cette** fille est sensas!

> **Ce** garçon est beau!

Demonstrative adjectives

Demonstrative adjectives are used when pointing things out, like 'this' and 'these' in English. Like all French adjectives, they have a different ending to match the masculine or feminine, singular or plural, of their noun.

This **ce** (when followed by a masculine singular word);
cet (when followed by a masculine singular word beginning with a vowel sound);
cette (when followed by a feminine singular word).

Note: Like **beau**, **nouveau** and **vieux**, with their alternative masculine singular forms **bel**, **nouvel** and **vieil**, **ce** becomes **cet**, to make it easier to say in front of a vowel sound.
Cet has the same pronunciation as the feminine singular form.

These **ces** (when followed by a masculine or feminine plural word).

The '**s**' of **ces** is silent, except when followed by a vowel sound, when it is used as a link.

Examples:
ce *matin* (m. s.)	this morning
cet *_après-midi* (m. s.)	this afternoon
cet *_homme* (m. s.)	this man
cette *année* (f. s.)	this year
ces *_endroits* (m. pl.)	these places
ces *villes* (f. pl.)	these towns

Practice 16.1

Possessive adjectives – my, your, his/her/its

Remember? **Possessive adjectives** show what belongs to which owner. (See Chapter 4, page 9.) They are useful to make your message more precise.

In French, the possessive adjective belongs to the person or thing possessed, NOT to the owner. This means that, whereas there is one possessive word in English, there is a choice of words in French.

My	**mon** (when followed by a masculine singular)
	ma* (when followed by a feminine singular)
	mes (when followed by a masculine or feminine plural)
Your (familiar singular)	**ton** (when followed by a masculine singular)
	ta* (when followed by a feminine singular)
	tes (when followed by a masculine or feminine plural)

This also means that **his**, **her** and **its** are the same words in French.

His, her, its	**son** (when followed by a masculine singular)
	sa* (when followed by a feminine singular)
	ses (when followed by a masculine or feminine plural)

Practice 16.2

☗ *Note: When **ma, ta, sa** come before a vowel sound, they change to **mon, ton, son**. This makes them easier to say. There is no such problem with *mon, ton, son, mes, tes or ses,* as their final '**–n**' or '**–s**' sound becomes a linking sound when they are followed by a vowel sound.

Examples:

mon_agenda (m. s.)	my diary
mes_agendas (m. pl.)	my diaries
mon_adresse mail (f. s.)	my e-mail address
mes_adresses mail (f. pl.)	my e-mail addresses
ton_ami Robert (m. s.)	your friend Robert
ton_amie Serena (f. s.)	your friend Serena
son_ami Robert (m. s.)	his/her friend Robert
son_amie Serena (f. s.)	his/her friend Serena

Practice 16.3

Possessive adjectives – our, your, their

☺ Saying 'our', 'your' (formal or plural), and 'their' is easier, as they have only two forms each.

Our	**notre** (when followed by a masculine or feminine singular);
	nos (when followed by a masculine or feminine plural).

The '**s**' of **nos** is silent, except when followed by a vowel sound, when it is used as a link.

Examples:

notre *père* (m. s.)	our father
notre *maison* (f. s.)	our house
nos_*amis* (m. pl.)	our friends
nos *tantes* (f. pl.)	our aunts

Practice 16.4

Your (formal/plural) *votre* (when followed by a masculine or feminine singular)
vos (when followed by a masculine or feminine plural)

The '*s*' of *vos* is silent, except when followed by a vowel sound, when it is used as a link.

Examples:
votre frère (m. s.)	your brother
votre voiture (f. s.)	your car
vos vêtements (m. pl.)	your clothes
*vos*_affaires (f. pl.)	your belongings

Practice 16.5

Their *leur* (when followed by a masculine or feminine singular)
leurs (when followed by a masculine or feminine plural)

Both forms have the same sound, except when followed by a vowel sound, when the '*s*' of *leurs* is used as a link.

Examples:
leur oncle (m. s.)	their uncle
leur chambre (f. s.)	their room
*leurs*_animaux (m. pl.)	their pets
leurs tantes (f. pl.)	their aunts

Practice 16.6 to 16.8

Chapter 17: | Adverbs

 ## Understand French grammar easily!

Remember? An **adverb** acts as a secretary to a verb, describing it (just as an adjective describes a noun). See Chapter 1, page 3.

How to make adverbs from adjectives

Most adverbs are formed by adding an ending to an adjective.
In English, the ending is usually '**–ly**'. In French, '**–ment**' is usually added to the feminine form of the adjective. Using the shorter masculine form would be too difficult to say.

Examples:			
Adjective		**Adverb**	
*lent – lent**e***	slow	*lent**e**ment*	slowly
*immédiat – immédiat**e***	immediate	*immédiat**e**ment*	immediately
*rare – rar**e***	rare	*rar**e**ment*	rarely

Adjectives ending in '**–ant**' or '**–ent**' and the adjective **gentil** become shorter, to make them easier to say. This does not apply to **lent**, which would almost disappear!

Examples:			
Adjective		**Adverb**	
bruyant – bruyam...	noisy	*bruyam**ment***	noisily
évident – évidem...	evident	*évidem**ment***	evidently
gentil – genti...	nice / kind	*gent**i**ment*	nicely / kindly

 Practice 17.1

 ## Irregular adverbs

A few adverbs do not end in '**–ment**'. These forms just have to be learnt.

Examples:

bien	well
mal	badly
mieux	better (as in 'he is better', not 'a better day' where 'better' is an adjective)
beaucoup	a lot / much
peu	a little / not much
souvent	often
vite	fast / quickly

Note: **bien** is used a lot in French to reinforce what you are saying. This happens not only with verbs, but also with adjectives.

Examples:

bien	well / much / truly
bien sûr	of course
bien entendu	it goes without saying (literally 'well heard')
bientôt	soon
ça va bien	it's fine, I am well
ça te va bien	it suits you (literally 'it goes well on you')
je veux bien	I'd like that (literally 'I really want')
vous êtes bien M. Mort?	you **are** Mr Mort, aren't you?

Oui, je vous entends bien … Bien sûr, je vais arriver bientôt! … Oui, je veux bien déjeuner avec vous … Oui, ça va bien … eh bien, hier, il y avait bien des problèmes, mais aujourd'hui ils sont bien en main. Je suis bien content!

'Yes, I can hear you well … Well sure, I'm going to arrive well early! … Yes, I well want to have lunch with you … Yes, it's going well. Oh well, yesterday, there well were problems, but today they are well in hand. I'm well pleased!'

Practice 17.2

Chapter 18: | Reflexive verbs

CD 57

Help yourself!

The word 'reflexive' comes from reflection, because the action comes back to the subject, just as a reflection in a mirror comes back to the person.

Quand **je m'**ennuie,
je me regarde dans un miroir,
et **je me** mords la queue.
Je m'amuse bien!'

'When **I get** bored, **I** look at **myself** in a mirror, and **I** bite **my** tail. I enjoy **myself**!'

How are reflexive verbs formed?

Reflexive verbs have an extra word, called a **reflexive pronoun**, e.g. 'myself', 'yourself', etc. The verbs still have endings, as normal (see Chapter 5, page 11).

se laver	**to get washed** (literally: to wash oneself)			
Singular			**Plural**	
1st person	*je* **me** *lave*	I get washed	*nous* **nous** *lavons*	we get washed
2nd person	*tu* **te** *laves*	you get washed	*vous* **vous** *lavez*	you get washed
3rd person	*il/elle/on*	he/she/one		
	se *lave*	gets washed	*ils/elles* **se** *lavent*	they get washed

The *me*, *te* and *se* shorten to *m'*, *t'* and *s'* before a vowel sound.

s'amuser	**to have a good time/to enjoy oneself** (literally: to amuse oneself)			
Singular			**Plural**	
1st person	*je* **m'**amuse	I have a good time	*nous* **nous** *amusons*	we have a good time
2nd person	*tu* **t'**amuses	you have a good time	*vous* **vous** *amusez*	you have a good time
3rd person	*il/elle/on*	he/she/one		
	s'amuse	has a good time	*ils/elles* **s'**amusent	they have a good time

Practice 18.1

When is a reflexive verb used?

A reflexive verb is used whenever the meaning is that the action comes back to the subject. The same verb can be used reflexively at times, and non-reflexively at other times, depending on the type of action.

Examples:

*Jackie **se lave**.*	Jackie washes her**self** (gets washed).
Jackie lave son fils.	Jackie washes her son.
*Elle **se regarde** dans le miroir.*	She looks at **herself** in the mirror.
Elle regarde une carte.	She looks at a map.

Practice 18.2

*Pour la Saint Valentin, Christine **envoie** une carte à Ian, mais Ian n'**envoie** pas de carte à Christine. Nicole et Frank **s'envoient** une carte. Kevin **s'envoie** une carte, parce qu'il pense que personne ne va lui écrire!*

For Valentine's Day, Christine **sends** a card to Ian, but Ian does not **send** a card to Christine. Nicole and Frank **send each other** a card. Kevin **sends himself** a card, because he thinks nobody is going to write to him!

☺ The meaning of a verb shows whether it needs to be used reflexively, or non-reflexively.

Reflexive verbs used for reciprocal actions

Reflexive verbs are also used with the meaning of an action done by the subjects to each other.

Examples:

*Les enfants **se battent**.*	The children **are fighting**.
*Les deux amis **se téléphonent**.*	The two friends **phone each other**.
*Carolyn et David **se marient**.*	Carolyn and David **are getting married**.
*Est-ce que vous **vous disputez**?*	Do you **argue with each other**?

Practice 18.3

Chapter 19: More about the present tense

CD 59

More about verbs: regular and irregular

Remember? Most French **verbs** belong to the **–er** category (about 4000 verbs).

☺ Apart from **aller** they are predictable because they follow the same pattern (see Chapter 5, page 11).

The **–er** group gets larger all the time, as new verbs created to go with new inventions and technologies are nearly always **–er** verbs e.g. **surfer** sur l'internet, or **zapper** (to channel hop with the remote).

The next largest group are **–ir** verbs. About 300 are regular and 50 irregular.

The smallest group are **–re** verbs. About 50 are regular and 50 irregular.

Regular –ir verbs

Let's look at the verb **finir** as an example of a regular **–ir** verb:

finir = to finish

	Singular	Plural
1st person	je fin**is**	nous fin**issons**
2nd person	tu fin**is**	vous fin**issez**
3rd person	il/elle/on fin**it**	ils/elles fin**issent**

☺ Most **–ir** verbs follow this pattern (about 300), especially those based on an adjective with the meaning of 'getting increasingly' something.

D'année en année, je vieillis, mais aujourd'hui je rajeunis.

Examples:

Les enfants grandissent.	The children are getting taller.
Je brunis au soleil.	I'm turning brown in the sun.
Tu blanchis de peur.	You are turning white with fear.
Vous grossissez.	You are getting fatter.
Elle ne rajeunit pas.	She is not getting (any) younger.
Nous vieillissons.	We are getting older.

Every year I get older, but today I am getting younger.

Irregular –ir verbs: sortir

Some **–ir** verbs have shorter endings.

Let's look at the verb **sortir**:

sortir = to go out

	Singular	Plural
1st person	*je sors*	*nous sortons*
2nd person	*tu sors*	*vous sortez*
3rd person	*il/elle/on sort*	*ils/elles sortent*

☺ Most of the 50 or so irregular **–ir** verbs follow this pattern.

Practice 19.1

You have already learnt a very useful irregular **–ir** verb: **avoir** (see Chapter 5, page 13).

There are a few others with unexpected endings, such as **devoir, offrir, ouvrir, pouvoir, savoir, tenir, venir** and **vouloir**.

☺ As you will see, they all have regular **nous** and **vous** forms.

Irregular –ir verbs: venir, tenir

In the case of **venir** and **tenir**, an **–i** appears in most forms, to make them easier to say:

venir = to come

	Singular	Plural
1st person	*je viens*	*nous venons*
2nd person	*tu viens*	*vous venez*
3rd person	*il/elle/on vient*	*ils/elles viennent*

tenir = to hold

	Singular	Plural
1st person	*je tiens*	*nous tenons*
2nd person	*tu tiens*	*vous tenez*
3rd person	*il/elle/on tient*	*ils/elles tiennent*

☺ It is easy to learn these two together, as they follow exactly the same pattern.

Practice 19.2

CD 62

Irregular –ir verbs: devoir, savoir

With **devoir** and **savoir** a change of vowel in most forms makes them easier to say:

> **devoir** = to have to
>
> | | Singular | Plural |
> |---|---|---|
> | 1st person | *je dois* | *nous devons* |
> | 2nd person | *tu dois* | *vous devez* |
> | 3rd person | *il/elle/on doit* | *ils/elles doivent* |

> **savoir** = to know (how to)
>
> | | Singular | Plural |
> |---|---|---|
> | 1st person | *je sais* | *nous savons* |
> | 2nd person | *tu sais* | *vous savez* |
> | 3rd person | *il/elle/on sait* | *ils/elles savent* |

☺ It is easy to learn these two together, as they follow almost the same pattern.

 Practice 19.3

CD 63

Irregular –ir verbs: pouvoir, vouloir

A similar change happens with **pouvoir** and **vouloir**:

> **pouvoir** = to be able to
>
> | | Singular | Plural |
> |---|---|---|
> | 1st person | *je peux* | *nous pouvons* |
> | 2nd person | *tu peux* | *vous pouvez* |
> | 3rd person | *il/elle/on peut* | *ils/elles peuvent* |

> **vouloir** = to want
>
> | | Singular | Plural |
> |---|---|---|
> | 1st person | *je veux* | *nous voulons* |
> | 2nd person | *tu veux* | *vous voulez* |
> | 3rd person | *il/elle/on veut* | *ils/elles veulent* |

☺ It is easy to learn these two together, as they follow exactly the same pattern.

Practice 19.4

Irregular –ir verbs: offrir, ouvrir

The verbs **offrir** and **ouvrir** pretend to be **–er** verbs:

offrir = to offer / give as a present

	Singular	Plural
1st person	j'offre	nous offrons
2nd person	tu offres	vous offrez
3rd person	il/elle/on offre	ils/elles offrent

ouvrir = to open

	Singular	Plural
1st person	j'ouvre	nous ouvrons
2nd person	tu ouvres	vous ouvrez
3rd person	il/elle/on ouvre	ils/elles ouvrent

☺ It is easy to learn these two together, as they follow exactly the same pattern.

Practice 19.5

Regular –re verbs

Let's look at the verb **attendre** as an example of a regular **–re** verb:

attendre = to wait

	Singular	Plural
1st person	j'attends	nous attendons
2nd person	tu attends	vous attendez
3rd person	il/elle/on attend	ils/elles attendent

Practice 19.6

You can see that it follows a similar pattern to **sortir**.

☺ About half of **–re** verbs do not follow the pattern of **attendre** exactly, but mostly they have only minor differences.

You have already learnt two slightly irregular **–re** verbs: **faire** = to do / make, and **prendre** = to take (see Chapter 5, page 14).

You have also learnt a very useful and very irregular **–re** verb: **être** = to be (see Chapter 5, page 13).

Practice 19.7

Irregular –re verbs: boire – dire

Here are two more that are really useful.

boire = to drink

	Singular	Plural
1st person	*je bois*	*nous b**uv**ons*
2nd person	*tu bois*	*vous b**uv**ez*
3rd person	*il/elle/on boit*	*ils/elles boi**v**ent*

dire = to say

	Singular	Plural
1st person	*je dis*	*nous disons*
2nd person	*tu dis*	*vous di**tes***
3rd person	*il/elle/on dit*	*ils/elles disent*

☺ Notice how similar **boire** is to **devoir** and **savoir**, and how similar **dire** is to **faire** (see Chapter 5, page 14).

Practice 19.8

Chapter 20: | More about the future tense

It will be easy!

Remember? An easy way of expressing things in the **future** is to say that you are 'going to' do them, with the verb **aller** + a verb in the infinitive (see Chapter 6, page 16).

Tes rides **disparaîtront**, mais Blanche Neige **sera** toujours la plus belle!

Miroir, miroir, comment est-ce que je **serai** après la chirurgie esthétique?

Examples:
Je vais voyager en Espagne.	I am going to travel to Spain.
Elle va travailler à Paris.	She is going to work in Paris.
Nous allons voir un film.	We are going to see a film.

As in English, however, there is another way of expressing future actions:

Examples:
*Je **voyagerai** en Espagne.*	I **shall travel** to Spain.
*Elle **travaillera** à Paris.*	She **will work** in Paris.
*Nous **verrons** un film.*	We **shall see** a film.

'Mirror, mirror, what will I be like after the cosmetic surgery?'

'Your wrinkles will disappear, but Snow White will always be the most beautiful!'

This is the 'real' future tense. In English it is formed by saying: 'I shall' or 'will' do something. It sounds more determined than saying 'I'm going to …'.
Note that, in correct English, 'shall' is used with the 1st persons and 'will' with the 2nd and 3rd persons.

How to form the future tense of most verbs

Let's look at an **–er** verb: **jouer** in the future tense:

jouer = to play

	Singular		Plural	
1st person	*je jouerai*	I shall play	*nous jouerons*	we shall play
2nd person	*tu joueras*	you will play	*vous jouerez*	you will play
3rd person	*il/elle/on jouera*	he/she/one will play	*ils/elles joueront*	they will play

In French, it is not formed by adding a word, but by adding endings to the infinitive.

☺ As you can see, the endings are those of **avoir** in the present:

j'ai, tu as, il/on a, nous (av)ons, vous (av)ez, ils/elles ont.

☺ **–ir** verbs do exactly the same, and **–re** verbs lose their **–e** before doing the same:

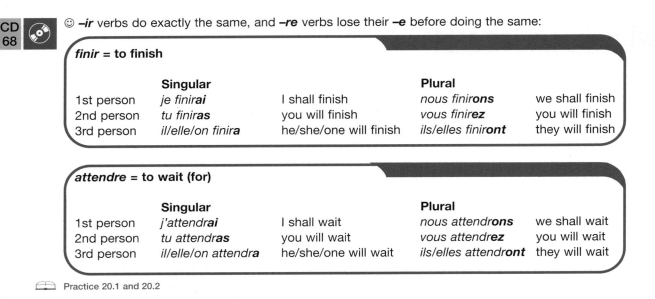

finir = to finish

	Singular		**Plural**	
1st person	*je finir**ai***	I shall finish	*nous finir**ons***	we shall finish
2nd person	*tu finir**as***	you will finish	*vous finir**ez***	you will finish
3rd person	*il/elle/on finir**a***	he/she/one will finish	*ils/elles finir**ont***	they will finish

attendre = to wait (for)

	Singular		**Plural**	
1st person	*j'attendr**ai***	I shall wait	*nous attendr**ons***	we shall wait
2nd person	*tu attendr**as***	you will wait	*vous attendr**ez***	you will wait
3rd person	*il/elle/on attendr**a***	he/she/one will wait	*ils/elles attendr**ont***	they will wait

Practice 20.1 and 20.2

Irregular verbs in the future tense

☺ Good news! The above endings are still the same, even for irregular verbs. Once you know the *je* form, the others are easy to work out.

☺ More good news! As with other tenses, **–er** verbs (apart from **aller** and a few spelling oddities) are all **regular**.

A small number of **–ir** verbs are irregular in the future. The ones that are irregular have become so to make them quicker to say. They are like a shorter version of what would be their regular form. They are still easy to recognise:

Examples:

avoir	→	*j'aurai*	I shall have
devoir	→	*je devrai*	I shall have to
faire	→	*je ferai*	I shall do
pouvoir	→	*je pourrai*	I shall be able to
savoir	→	*je saurai*	I shall know (how to)
venir	→	*je viendrai*	I shall come
voir	→	*je verrai*	I shall see
vouloir	→	*je voudrai*	I shall want

Practice 20.3

♟ There are two verbs which are really irregular in the future tense. They are difficult to recognise, but they still add the same endings as all the other verbs:

aller = to go

	Singular		Plural	
1st person	j'**ir**ai	I shall go	nous **ir**ons	we shall go
2nd person	tu **ir**as	you will go	vous **ir**ez	you will go
3rd person	il/elle/on **ir**a	he/she/one will go	ils/elles **ir**ont	they will go

être = to be

	Singular		Plural	
1st person	je **ser**ai	I shall be	nous **ser**ons	we shall be
2nd person	tu **ser**as	you will be	vous **ser**ez	you will be
3rd person	il/elle/on **ser**a	he/she/one will be	ils/elles **ser**ont	they will be

☺ All verbs in the future tense have the letter '**r**' immediately before the endings. It has a strong gargling sound in French, making it easy to recognise.

Practice 20.4 to 20.7

Chapter 21: More about the perfect tense

Past participles

Remember? The **perfect tense** is the main past tense in French. (See Chapter 8, page 19)

☺ For most verbs it is formed in the same way as in English:

Examples:

I have played	He has liked	They have decided
↓ ↓	↓ ↓	↓ ↓
J'ai joué	*Il a aimé*	*Elles ont décidé*

As you can see, you start to form the perfect tense with the present tense of **avoir** (called the **auxiliary**). Then use the verb you need, changing the '**–er**', of its infinitive to '**–é**' (this form is called the **past participle**).

Practice 21.1

But, of course, not all verbs are **–er** verbs, so what happens to the others?

Past participle recipe

1. For **–er** verbs: '**–er**' always becomes '**–é**'. Pronounce the '**–é**' with a half smile.

90% of French verbs are of this type.

Examples:

chercher	→	j'ai cher**ché**	I (have) looked for
manger	→	elle a man**gé**	I ate/have eaten
écouter	→	nous avons écou**té**	we (have) heard

Practice 21.2

Recipe card
French-style perfect tense
Ingredients:
- 1 auxiliary (avoir or être)
- 1 verb (of your choice)
Method
- Take the auxiliary, making sure you have its correct endings
- Trim the verb, to obtain its past participle
- Add the past participle to the auxiliary
Et voilà! You now have a perfect tense!

---

2. For *–ir* verbs: '*–ir*' becomes '*–i*'. Pronounce the '*–i*' with a full smile.

There are quite a few exceptions, most of them ending in '*–u*:'

Examples:			
finir	→	*tu as fini*	you (have) finished
choisir	→	*vous avez choisi*	you chose / have chosen
but:			
a**voir**	→	*il a eu*	he (has) had
de**voir**	→	*ils ont dû*	they (have) had to
pleu**voir**	→	*il a plu*	it (has) rained
pou**voir**	→	*j'ai pu*	I have been / was able to
rece**voir**	→	*elle a reçu*	she (has) received
voir	→	*il a vu*	he saw / has seen
and:			
vouloir	→	*elles ont voulu*	they (have) wanted
courir	→	*tu as couru*	you ran / have run
tenir	→	*on a tenu*	one (has) held
and:			
ouvrir	→	*elle a ouvert*	she (has) opened

   Practice 21.3

☺ Note that most of the irregular verbs end in '*–voir*', and have a very short past participle ending in '*–u*'. Pronounce the '*–u*' as a whistle.

3. For *–re* verbs: '*–re*' becomes '*–u*'.

There are quite a few exceptions, often with a shortened form in '*–u*', '*–t*' or '*–s*':

Examples:			
attendre	→	*elle a attendu*	she (has) waited (for)
répondre	→	*il a répondu*	he (has) answered
but:			
boire	→	*nous avons bu*	we drank / have drunk
croire	→	*vous avez cru*	you (have) believed
lire	→	*tu as lu*	you (have) read
dire	→	*j'ai dit*	I (have) said
faire	→	*vous avez fait*	you did / have done
écrire	→	*elle a écrit*	she wrote / has written
mettre	→	*j'ai mis*	I (have) put
prendre	→	*ils ont pris*	they took / have taken
and:			
être	→	*j'ai été*	I was / have been

   Practice 21.4

There are quite a few exceptions in English too; not all past participles end in **–ed** (e.g. eaten, spoken, seen, sung, read, gone, bought, etc.).

   Practice 21.5

Chapter 22: | *Still more about the perfect tense!*

CD 74

Verbs that take être

Remember the perfect tense of **aller** (see Chapter 8, page 21)?

A small number of verbs start their perfect tense with a part of the present of **être** instead of **avoir**. This happens with all verbs used reflexively (see Chapter 18, page 51) and a few non-reflexive verbs such as **aller**:

aller = to go

	Singular		Plural	
1st person	*je suis allé(e)**	I went	*nous sommes allé(e)s**	we went
2nd person	*tu es allé(e)**	you went	*vous êtes allé(e)s**	you went
3rd person	*il est allé*	he/it went	*ils sont allés*	they (m.) went
	elle est allée	she/it went	*elles sont allées*	they (f.) went

Are you wondering why there is an extra '–e*' or '*–s*'? It is explained in the section on **the past participle agreement**, page 64.

Why être instead of avoir?

Remember about subjects and objects (see Chapter 12, page 29)? Verbs forming their perfect tense with **être** cannot be followed by an object; the action they express either comes back to the subject (for reflexive verbs), or does not go anywhere (for the few other verbs).

By contrast, the majority of verbs have the ability to lead to an object (even if no object is actually there). They are the ones forming their perfect tense with **avoir**:

Examples:

J'ai aimé le film.	I liked the film.
Est-ce que tu as fini ton livre?	Have you finished your book?
Elle a parlé à son frère.	She spoke to her brother.
*Il s'**est** lavé.*	He got washed.
*Nous nous **sommes** habillé(e)s.*	We got dressed.
*Elle s'**est** amusée.*	She enjoyed herself.
*Vous **êtes** parti(e)(s).*	You left.
*Ils **sont** arrivés.*	They arrived.
*Elles **sont** rentrées.*	They came back.

Many of the verbs that cannot be followed by an object express a 'personal movement':

aller = ('to go')	*venir* = ('to come')
arriver = ('to arrive')	*partir* = ('to leave')
(r)entrer = ('to come in')	*sortir* = ('to go out')
monter = ('to go up')	*descendre* = ('to go/come down')
tomber = ('to fall')	
	but also: *rester* = ('to stay')
naître = ('to be born'),	*mourir* = ('to die')

Three of these have an irregular past participle: *venir* → *venu; naître* → *né; mourir* → *mort.*

 Practice 22.1

Verbs taking être at times and avoir at other times

Some of the ***être*** verbs have a second meaning of 'moving something', rather than a 'personal movement'. In such cases, they are no longer ***être*** verbs, but ***avoir*** verbs.

> Bond **est** descendu de l'hélicoptère et il **a** descendu le criminel.
>
> Bond came down from the helicopter and gunned down the criminal.

Examples:

*Je **suis** sorti dans la rue.*	I went out into the street.
*J'**ai** sorti mon chien.*	I took my dog out.
*Elle **est** descendue.*	She came down.
*Elle **a** descendu sa valise.*	She brought her case down.
*Il **est** rentré au garage.*	He went into the garage.
*Il **a** rentré sa voiture au garage.*	He put his car in the garage.

In the same way, a verb can be used reflexively, in which case it is an ***être*** verb in the perfect tense, or not reflexively, in which case it is an ***avoir*** verb. (See Chapter 18 page 51.)

Examples:

*Je **me suis lavé(e)**.*	I got washed.
*J'**ai lavé** la vaisselle.*	I washed the dishes.
*Il **s'est réveillé**.*	He woke up.
*Elle **a réveillé** sa cousine.*	She woke up her cousin.

 Practice 22.2

The past participle agreement

Although a past participle is a form coming from a verb, it is in fact an adjective. This is also the case in English (e.g. 'tired', 'contented', 'amused', 'bored').

This explains why, as you can see in the examples for the previous section, you have to add an '*e*' (for feminine) or an '*s*' (for plural) to the end of the past participle, just as you do with French adjectives. This happens for verbs forming their perfect tense with *être*, and only in very rare cases for those forming their perfect tense with *avoir*:

Examples:

Il s'est lavé.	He (masc.sing.) got washed.
Elle s'est lavée.	She (fem.sing.) got washed.
Je me suis habillé.	I (masc.sing.) got dressed.
Nous nous sommes habillés.	We (masc.pl.) got dressed.
Elle est partie.	She (fem.sing.) left.
Elles sont parties.	They (fem.pl.) left.
Il est arrivé.	He (masc.sing.) arrived.
Ils sont arrivés.	They (masc.pl.) arrived.

Practice 22.3 and 22.4

The precise rules of the past participle agreement are very complex. Many native French speakers make mistakes when using the perfect tense, so don't worry if you find it difficult!

A final note: to say 'after having …' in French, use *après avoir* or *après être* + past participle, following exactly the same procedure as for the perfect tense (choosing the auxiliary but leaving it in the infinitive, then adding the past participle, with an agreement for *être* verbs). This is called a **perfect infinitive**:

Examples:

Après avoir mangé, elle est rentrée.	After having eaten, she returned home.
Après être rentrée, elle s'est reposée.	After having returned, she had a rest.
Après s'être reposée, elle a travaillé.	After having rested, she worked.

Chapter 23: | The imperfect tense

Why another past tense?

All verbs can be used sometimes in the perfect, sometimes in the imperfect, depending on the circumstances. The perfect shows a finished, completed action, the imperfect an unfinished, incomplete action, or something that was done repeatedly or regularly, or 'used to be' done.

A message in the past relates something that happened (the story line), but to make it more understandable, details (of the location, time, who was involved, what was going on, or what happened routinely) are often provided as background information:

Examples:

Story line	**Background information**
	As it was raining last weekend,
I decided to go to the cinema.	
I called my friend.	
	She was free,
so she came with me.	
We went on the bus.	
We saw the latest 'James Bond'.	
	It was great!
	Because the film finished late,
we asked my mother to pick us up.	
	Before, she used to drive very fast,
but since she had an accident last year, she has slowed down a lot.	

Here is the same story in French:

Story line	**Background information**
	*Comme il **pleuvait** le weekend dernier,*
*j'**ai décidé** d'aller au cinéma.*	
*J'**ai appelé** mon amie.*	
	*Elle **était** libre,*
*donc elle **est venue** avec moi.*	
*Nous **sommes allé(e)s** en autobus.*	
*Nous **avons vu** le dernier 'James Bond'.*	
	*C'**était** formidable!*
	*Comme le film **finissait** tard,*
*nous **avons demandé** à ma mère de venir nous chercher.*	
	*Avant, elle **conduisait** très vite,*
*mais depuis qu'elle **a eu** un accident l'année dernière, elle **a** beaucoup **ralenti**.*	

The story line is expressed in the **perfect**, whereas the background information is in the **imperfect**.

Practice 23.1

☺ This explains why **être** and **avoir** are found more often in the imperfect than the perfect (see Chapter 8, page 21). The same applies to weather phrases and descriptions, as they are more likely to provide background information than to be the story line. Similarly, the phrase **pendant que** (while) is always followed by the imperfect tense rather than the perfect, for the same reason.

How is the imperfect tense formed?

☺ It is the easiest tense of all to form!

Let's look at the verb **jouer** in the imperfect:

jouer = to play

	Singular		Plural	
1st person	*je jouais*	I was playing/ used to play/played	*nous jouions*	we were playing, etc.
2nd person	*tu jouais*	you were playing, etc.	*vous jouiez*	you were playing, etc.
3rd person	*il/elle jouait*	he/she/it was playing, etc.	*ils/elles jouaient*	they were playing, etc.

☺ Most of the endings sound the same.
Apart from the **nous** and **vous** forms, they all have the same long '**–ai**' sound (the same as **è**).

This sounds very different from the short, half-smile '**é**' sound found in the perfect tense.
Compare **je jouais** (imperfect), with **j'ai joué** (perfect).

☺ The endings are the same for **all** verbs. They replace the '**–ons**' of the **nous** form of the present tense.

Examples:

infinitive		nous form		imperfect	
jouer	→	nous **jou**ons	→	je **jou**ais	I was playing/used to play/played, etc.
prendre	→	nous **pren**ons	→	nous **pren**ions	we were taking, etc.
finir	→	nous **finiss**ons	→	tu **finiss**ais	you were finishing, etc.
boire	→	nous **buv**ons	→	il **buv**ait	he was drinking, etc.
avoir	→	nous **av**ons	→	vous **av**iez	you were having, etc.

> Try this tongue twister: *je choisissais, tu choisissais, il choisissait, nous choisissions, vous choisissiez, ils choisissaient.*

☺ For all **–er** verbs and most other verbs, it is the same as having the endings instead of the '**–er**', '**–ir**', or '**–re**' of the infinitive. This can be a handy shortcut.

Practice 23.2 to 23.6

Chapter 24: More about questions

Are there other ways to ask them?

Remember? An easy way of turning a statement into a **question** is to put *est-ce que* in front of it (see Chapter 9, page 23).

☺ This is the easiest and, increasingly, the most popular way of forming questions.

There are two other ways: changing the way you say it (intonation) and changing the words round (inversion).

Asking questions with intonation only

A question can be asked simply by raising the voice at the end of the sentence. Try and raise your shoulders at the same time.

This is called **intonation**.

This type of question is quite familiar. It is fine to use in speaking, but not really suitable for writing.

'Yes, you say that. But you say that, why?'

Examples:

question with *'est-ce que'*	question raising the voice
Est-ce que Mike avait son baladeur? Did Mike have his walkman?	*Mike avait son baladeur?*
Est-ce qu'il a acheté un lecteur de CD? Has he bought a CD player?	*Il a acheté un lecteur de CD?*
Est-ce qu'il est chez lui? Is he at home?	*Il est chez lui?*
Est-ce qu'il écoute sa musique? Is he listening to his music?	*Il écoute sa musique?*
Est-ce que ses parents veulent qu'il s'arrête? Do his parents want him to stop?	*Ses parents veulent qu'il s'arrête?*

Practice 24.1

This can also be done when a precise question word is used, but then the question word is no longer at the beginning of the question.

Examples:

Où *est-ce que tu as acheté ton pull?* Where did you buy your jumper?	*Tu as acheté ton pull* **où**?
Quand *est-ce que c'était?* When was it?	*C' était* **quand**?
Comment *est-ce que tu as payé?* How did you pay?	*Tu as payé* **comment**?
Qu'est-ce *que tu vas mettre avec?* What are you going to wear with it?	**Tu vas mettre* **quoi** *avec*?
Quelle couleur *est-ce que tu préfères?* Which / what colour do you prefer?	*Tu préfères* **quelle** *couleur*?
Combien *est-ce que tu as* **de** *pulls noirs?* How many black jumpers do you have?	*Tu as* **combien de** *pulls noirs*?
Pourquoi *est-ce que tu en as acheté un noir?* Why did you buy a black one?	*Tu en as acheté un noir,* **pourquoi**?
Avec qui *est-ce que tu vas à la fête?* Who are you going to the party with?	*Tu vas à la fête* **avec qui**?
Combien de temps *est-ce que tu vas rester?* How long are you going to stay?	*Tu vas rester* **combien de temps**?

*Note: **que / qu'** *changes to* **quoi** *in this type of question form.*

Practice 24.2

Asking questions with inversion

A third way of asking a question is by changing the order of the verb and its subject in the sentence. This is called **inversion**. This also happens with certain verbs in English (e.g. You are → Are you?   He has → Has he?   They did → Did they?)

This way is more formal and used less and less in French, except in the perfect tense (because it is shorter), but it is useful for written messages.

Examples:

Où est-ce que **tu as** *acheté ton pull?* Where did you buy your jumper?	*Où* **as-tu** *acheté ton pull?*
Quand est-ce que **c'était**? When was it?	*Quand* **était-ce**?
Comment est-ce que **tu as** *payé?* How did you pay?	*Comment* **as-tu** *payé?*
Qu'est-ce que **tu vas** *mettre avec?* What are you going to wear with it?	*Que* **vas-tu** *mettre avec?*
Quelle couleur est-ce que **tu préfères**? Which colour do you prefer?	*Quelle couleur* **préfères-tu**?
Combien est-ce que **tu as** *de pulls noirs?* How many black jumpers do you have?	*Combien de pulls noirs* **as-tu**?

*Pourquoi est-ce que **tu** en **as** acheté un noir?*
Why did you buy a black one?

*Pourquoi en **as-tu** acheté un noir?*

*Avec qui est-ce que **tu vas** à la fête?*
Who are you going to the party with?

*Avec qui **vas-tu** à la fête?*

*Combien de temps est-ce que **tu vas** rester?*
How long are you going to stay?

*Combien de temps **vas-tu** rester?*

Practice 24.3

Three points to note about inversion questions

1. The inversion cannot normally be used with the *je* form; it is only possible with:

avoir	→	*ai-je?*	have I?
être	→	*suis-je?*	am I?

And, rarely, with:

aller	→	*vais-je?*	do I go?
dire	→	*dis-je?*	do I say?
faire	→	*fais-je?*	do I do / make?
pouvoir	→	*puis-je?*	may I? (notice the strange **puis** form)

Examples:

*Où est-ce que **je suis**?*
Where am I?

*Où **suis-je**?*

*Est-ce que **j'ai** bien entendu?*
Did I hear properly?

***Ai-je** bien entendu?*

Qu'est-ce que je vais faire?
What am I going to do?

*Que **vais-je** faire?*

Comment est-ce que je sors d'ici?
How do I get out of here?

(inversion not possible)

2. To avoid having a clash between vowel sounds, a '*-t-*' is added between a verb ending in a vowel and *il, elle* or *on*, as a linking sound:

Examples:

*Où va-**t**-il?* — Where is he going?
*A-**t**-elle fini?* — Has she finished?
*Pourquoi fume-**t**-on?* — Why do people smoke?

3. When the subject is a noun (rather than a pronoun), it is not possible to invert the verb and its subject. Instead a pronoun *(il / elle / ils / elles)* has to be used, as well as the noun:

Examples:

*Quel sport est-ce que **Jean préfère**?*
Which sport does Jean prefer?

***Jean**, quel sport préfère-t-**il**?*

*Est-ce que **les joueurs** portent un uniforme?*
Do the players wear a uniform?

***Les joueurs**, portent-**ils** un uniforme?*

*Pourquoi est-ce que **les actrices** sont si riches?*
Why are actresses so wealthy?

***Les actrices**, pourquoi sont-**elles** si riches?*

*Où est-ce que **Sophia** habite?*
Where does Sophia live?

*Sophia, où habite-t-**elle**?*

Practice 24.4

☺ So the ***est-ce que*** form is much easier to use than the inversion method.

Nous sommes les meilleurs, n'est-ce pas?

'We are the best, innit?'

The question ***n'est-ce pas***? can be put on the end of a statement to confirm it:

Examples:
*Les Français mangent des huîtres pour Noël, **n'est-ce pas**?*
The French eat oysters for Christmas, **don't they**?

*Tu aimes les escargots, **n'est-ce pas**?*
You do like snails, **don't you**?

*Et tu vas essayer les cuisses de grenouille aussi, **n'est-ce pas**?*
And you will try frogs' legs as well, **won't you**?

Practice 24.5

Chapter 25: More about negatives

'Never', 'nobody', 'no more', 'nothing' and 'only'

☺ Remember? It is easy to say **not** in French – much easier than in English. It is like making a verb sandwich, with the negative words **ne** (**n'** before a vowel sound) and **pas** acting as the two slices of bread (see Chapter 10, page 24).

*Mike **n'**aime **pas** le sport.*	Mike does not like sport.
*Il **ne** veut **pas** se fatiguer.*	He does not want to get tired.
*Il **ne** sort **pas** de chez lui.*	He does not go out of his home.

Practice 25.1

Similarly, to say 'never', 'nothing', 'nobody' etc, we use
ne / n' + *verb*, followed by a negative word (instead of *pas*):

ne / n' … jamais	never / not … ever
ne / n' … rien	nothing / not … anything
ne / n' … personne	nobody / not … anybody/ no-one/ not … anyone
ne / n' … plus	no more / not … any more / none left
ne / n' … nulle part	nowhere / not … anywhere
*ne / n' … que**	only

*Note: 'only' is not a negative in English, but it is in French. If you think about its meaning, it is half way between positive and negative (like 'nothing but').

'This bottle is half-empty!'
'No, it's only half-full!'

Examples:

*Mike **ne** joue **jamais** au football.*	Mike never plays football.
*Il **ne** fait **rien** le dimanche.*	He does nothing on Sundays.
*Il **n'**aime **personne**.*	He does not like anybody.
*Il **ne** va **plus** au cinéma.*	He does not go to the cinema any more.
*Il **ne** sort **nulle part**.*	He does not go out anywhere.
*Il **ne** parle **que** de musique.*	He talks only about music.
*Il **n'**a **plus** d'amis.*	He has no friends left.

Practice 25.2

Four things to note about negatives

1. Two negatives used together:
   In French, as in English, you can combine more than one negative idea in a sentence:

   Examples:

Mike **ne** regarde **plus rien** à la télé.	Mike does not watch anything on TV any more.
Il **n'**invite **jamais personne** chez lui.	He never invites anyone to his home.
Il **ne** voit **plus jamais personne.**	He never sees anyone any more.

2. Starting a sentence with a negative word:
   As in English, **rien** and **personne** are sometimes the first word of a sentence. In this case they are the subject:

   Examples:

Rien n'arrive.	Nothing is happening.
Personne ne vient chez lui.	Nobody comes to his home.

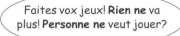

Faites vox jeux! **Rien ne** va plus! **Personne ne** veut jouer?

3. Negative replies:
   As in English, a negative word can by itself be a short reply to a question:

   Examples:

Qui a vu mes clés? – **Personne**.	Who's seen my keys? – Nobody.
Qu'est-ce que tu as mangé? – **Rien**.	What did you eat? – Nothing.
Tu es allé à Paris? – **Jamais**.	Have you been to Paris? – Never.
Où es-tu allé? – **Nulle part**.	Where did you go? – Nowhere.

4. The French often leave out the **ne/n'** in conversation:

   Examples:

Je sais **pas**.	I don't know.
Il l'a **jamais** vu.	He has never seen it.

   'Avant l'heure c'est pas l'heure; après l'heure c'est plus l'heure!'
   'Before the time it's not time; after the time it's no longer time!'

Practice 25.3

How to translate 'neither ... nor', 'not ... either'

When translating words such as 'neither' and 'nor', note that French uses what appears to be a double negative:

Examples:

Mike **ne** lit **ni** livres **ni** magazines.	Mike reads neither books nor magazines.
Ni la musique **ni** la peinture **n'**intéressent ce garçon.	Neither music nor painting interests this boy.
Il **n'**apprécie **pas** les journaux **non plus**.	He does not enjoy newspapers either.

Practice 25.4

Chapter 26: More about pronouns

A host of new pronouns

Remember? **Pronouns** replace nouns you don't want to repeat. We have already seen three kinds of pronouns: subject pronouns, object pronouns (see Chapter 12, page 29), and reflexive pronouns (see Chapter 18, page 50).

Direct and indirect object pronouns

In grammar, the object is the noun or pronoun affected by the action of the verb.

There are two types of objects: **direct** objects and **indirect** objects.

Direct simply means that you go directly from the verb to the object, e.g: Sean buys a ticket.

Indirect means that you need a preposition to introduce the object, therefore you go indirectly from the verb to the object, e.g. Sean gives the ticket **to** his brother.

Practice 26.1

Here are the lists of direct object and indirect object pronouns in French:

Direct object pronouns		Indirect object pronouns	
me/m' (+ vowel)	me	*me/m'* (+ vowel)	at/to/for me
te/t' (+ vowel)	you (familiar)	*te/t'* (+ vowel)	at/to/for you (familiar)
le/l' (+ vowel)	him	*lui*	at/to/for him
la/l' (+ vowel)	her	*lui*	at/to/for her
le (m.)/*la* (f.)/*l'* (+ vowel)	it	*lui*	at/to/for it
nous	us	*nous*	at/to/for us
vous	you (formal/plural)	*vous*	at/to/for you (formal/plural)
les	them	*leur*	at/to/for them

As you can see, some of the pronoun forms are shared: *me, te, nous* and ***vous*** can be direct objects, indirect objects, or reflexive pronouns. ***Nous*** and ***vous*** can also be subjects (see Chapter 12, page 29).

Whereas in English the indirect object pronouns are made up of 'at', 'to' or 'for' + the direct objects, in French the indirect object pronoun words already contain the idea of 'at', 'to' or 'for':

Examples:

Nicole **nous** appelle.	Nicole calls **us**.
Nicole **nous** parle.	Nicole speaks **to us**.
Nous allons **la** voir.	We are going to see **her**.
Nous **lui** écrivons un mail.	We write an e-mail **to her**.
Vous **les** emmenez au cinéma?	Are you taking **them** to the cinema?
Je **leur** achète des billets.	I buy tickets **for them**.
Ils **me** remercient.	They thank **me**.
Ils **me** donnent de l'argent.	They give some money **to me**.

Practice 26.2

Position of pronouns

Just as with the direct object pronouns, indirect object pronouns are placed before the verb in French (see Chapter 12, page 29).

This is still true in a negative sentence.

Examples:

J'ai écrit à Nicole.	I wrote to Nicole.
Je **lui** ai écrit.	I wrote to her.
Je ne **lui** ai pas écrit.	I did not write to her.

If there is a first verb followed by a second verb in the infinitive, the direct and indirect pronouns go in front of the verb they belong with.

Examples:

Je veux **lui** écrire.	I want to write to her.
Je vais **lui** écrire.	I am going to write to her.

Practice 26.3

Transitive or intransitive?

A **transitive verb** is one capable of having a **direct object** (there is direct transit from the verb to the object).

An **intransitive verb** cannot have a direct object (there is no direct transit from the verb to the object). It may or may not be capable of having an indirect object.

Most transitive English verbs are also transitive in French. Most intransitive English verbs are also intransitive in French. However, a few are different.

1. Transitive verbs in French that are intransitive in English.

For these, 'at', 'to' or 'for' is already contained within the French verb. Here are some of the most common ones: **regarder** (to look at), **écouter** (to listen to), **chercher** (to look for).

Examples:

*Nous **regardons** les magazines.*	We **look at** the magazines.
*Nous les **regardons**.*	We **look at** them.
*Je vais **écouter** la radio.*	I'm going to **listen to** the radio.
*Je vais l'**écouter**.*	I'm going to **listen to** it.
*Elle **cherche** sa clé.*	She is **looking for** her key.
*Elle la **cherche**.*	She is **looking for** it.

2. Intransitive verbs in French that are transitive in English.

Examples:

*Vous téléphonez **à** vos amis.*	You telephone your friends.
*Vous **leur** téléphonez.*	You telephone **them**.
*Ils ont répondu **à** leur mère.*	They answered their mother.
*Ils **lui** ont répondu.*	They answered **her**.
*Je vais demander **à** mon père.*	I am going to ask my father.
*Je vais **lui** demander.*	I am going to ask **him**.

Practice 26.4

Indirect objects in disguise

English indirect objects are sometimes 'in disguise' and difficult to distinguish from direct objects.

'He gave **his girlfriend** some chocolates'=
'He gave some chocolates **to his girlfriend**'.

'She bought **him** a watch' = 'She bought a watch **for him**'.

In the 'in disguise' construction, the direct and indirect objects are in reverse order, and the '**to**' or '**for**' are missed out. However, you can see that the direct object (the chocolates and the watch) is the first word that the verb happens to, whereas it can only happen to the indirect object ('his girlfriend' and 'him') afterwards.

This 'in disguise' construction does not happen in French.

"Il a donné son complice...les documents." Pourquoi donner son complice aux documents? Ça n'a pas de sens!

' "He gave his accomplice ... the documents." Why give his accomplice to the documents? It does not make sense!'

Examples:

Il a donné des chocolats à sa copine.	He gave his girlfriend some chocolates.
*Il **lui** a donné des chocolats.*	He gave her some chocolates.
*Elle **lui** a acheté une montre.*	She bought him a watch.

Practice 26.5

Emphatic pronouns

Whenever you need to emphasise that you are referring to one person rather than another, use an **emphatic pronoun**.

This happens with phrases expressing how something is related to someone:

Examples:

devant **moi**	in front of me
derrière **elle**	behind her
à côté de **lui**	next to him
pour **eux**	for them
avec **nous**	with us
avant **toi**	before you
à **elle**	belonging to her, hers
chez **vous**	to/at your place
sans **elles**	without them (feminine)

And they are also used in one word answers, singling a person out, or to start a sentence in an emphatic way:

Examples:

*Qui a dit ça? – Pas **moi**, **eux**!*	Who said this? – Not me, them!
*Qui va faire ce travail? – **Lui**!*	Who is going to do this work? – Him!
***Toi**, tu aimes bien danser.*	(As for) you, you like dancing a lot.
***Nous**, nous n'aimons pas ça du tout.*	(As for) us, we don't like it at all.

Here is the list of emphatic pronouns in French. These do not exist as a different set of pronouns in English:

moi	me
toi	you (familiar)
lui	him
elle	her
nous	us
vous	you (formal/plural)
eux	them (masculine)
elles	them (feminine)

Moi, petit moi!

As you can see, in English, the direct object pronouns are used, instead of a separate set of pronouns.

You have already met:

elle and **elles** as subject pronouns ('she' and 'they' feminine);
lui as an indirect object pronoun ('to/for him/her');
nous and **vous** as subject pronouns ('we' and 'you'), as reflexive pronouns ('ourselves' and 'yourselves'), as direct object pronouns ('us' and 'you'), and as indirect object pronouns ('to us' and 'to you').

Practice 26.6

Y and en

Two more little pronouns that you need to know are **y** and **en**:

> **y** is equivalent to the English 'there';
> **en** is equivalent to the English 'some'/'any'/'of it'/'of them'.

Like the direct object pronouns and the indirect object pronouns, they go before the verb.
Here, too, it is still the case with a negative sentence.

Examples:	
Elle **y** est allée.	She went there.
Elle n'**y** est pas allée.	She did not go there.
Il **y** a un cinéma au centre.	There is a cinema in the centre (literally: it has there).
Tu **en** as acheté.	You bought some (of it/of them).
J'**en** mange.	I eat some (of it/of them).
Je n'**en** mange pas.	I'm not eating any (of it/of them).
Ils **en** feront un petit peu.	They will do a little bit of it.

Note: In English the words 'of it'/'of them' are sometimes missed out. You cannot do this in French.

Examples:	
Tu **en** as acheté une.	You bought one (of them).
J'**en** mange beaucoup.	I eat a lot (of it/of them).
Il n'**en** trouve pas.	He can't find any (of it/them).

Practice 26.7 and 26.8

Relative pronouns qui and que/qu'

Relative pronouns are very useful to help you to improve your style. They link into one sentence what would otherwise have to be expressed in two.

In the following examples, you can see how the first version is repetitive. The second one is better, and the third is the most elegant.

Examples:	
J'ai un lézard. Le lézard ne mord pas.	I have a lizard. The lizard doesn't bite.
J'ai un lézard. Il ne mord pas.	I have a lizard. It doesn't bite.
J'ai un lézard **qui** ne mord pas.	I have a lizard which doesn't bite.
J'ai un serpent. J'aime bien le serpent.	I have a snake. I like the snake.
J'ai un serpent. Je l'aime bien.	I have a snake. I like it.
J'ai un serpent **que** j'aime bien.	I have a snake that I like.

Practice 26.9

Qui is used to replace a **subject** (like **il, elle, ils, elles**) and make a link with it.
Que is used to replace a **direct object** (like **le, la, l', les**) and make a link with it. **Que** shortens to **qu'** before a vowel sound.

Practice 26.10

Qui can be translated as 'who', 'which' or 'that'.
Que/qu' can be translated as 'whom', 'which' or 'that'. 'That' is often left out.

In English, 'who' and 'whom' are used for people; 'which' and 'that' are used for things or animals.

Practice 26.11 and 26.12

Et maintenant, bonne chance!

Practice Exercises

Chapter 1

Practice 1.1

Are these words verbs or nouns? Write V or N, then give the English meaning:

Example:

sortir ⇒ V = to go out

1. *cinéma*
2. *regarder*
3. *billet*
4. *places*
5. *rentrer*
6. *film*

Practice 1.2

Choose one word from those in brackets to complete each sentence, and show what part of speech it is. Then give the English meaning:

Example:

Il prend une ...... glace. (est / grande / aussi) ⇒ ***grande*** – adjective = 'He has a big ice-cream.'

1. *Je mange ...... gâteau. (le / avec / bleu)*
2. *Elle aime les ...... (dans / bonbons / achète)*
3. *Vous ...... le poisson ou le poulet? (préférez / je / mais)*
4. *Voici une ...... boîte de chocolats pour vous. (avant / la / grande)*
5. *Il commande une pizza ...... un coca. (sur / aime / et)*
6. *Nous allons ...... restaurant. (au / grand / ils)*
7. *Et toi, ... aimes le café? (thé / avec / tu)*
8. *Elles lisent ...... (silencieusement / bon / derrière)*

Practice 1.3

Show what parts of speech are in these sentences:

Example:

Je suis anglaise. ⇒ pronoun, verb, adjective.

1. *Eric habite Marseille.*
2. *Il a une grande maison.*
3. *Elle est située près de la mer.*
4. *Eric aime aller à la plage.*
5. *Il joue avec son chien.*

Practice 1.4

Unjumble the following sentences:

Example:

croissant mange Elle un ⇒ *Elle mange un croissant.*

1. *Tour La est Eiffel formidable.*
2. *fait le sud Il dans beau.*
3. *France la la Paris est capitale de.*
4. *J' musique italienne la aime.*
5. *copains mes vacances avec Je en pars.*

Chapter 2

Practice 2.1

Show whether the following nouns are likely to be masculine or feminine, and which are hard to tell:

Example:
chien ⇒ M, *répétition* ⇒ F, *cuisine* ⇒ ?

1. *éléphant*
2. *girafe*
3. *télévision*
4. *football*
5. *réaction*
6. *voiture*
7. *France*
8. *Brésil*
9. *bus*
10. *docteur*

Practice 2.2

Write that there are two of these and then give the English meanings:

Example: *un train* = a train ⇒ *deux trains* = two trains

1. *un avion*
2. *une voiture*
3. *un hélicoptère*
4. *un vélo*
5. *une mobylette*

Practice 2.3

Write these singular words in the plural, then give the English meaning:

Example: *le chapeau* ⇒ *les chapeaux* = the hats

1. *le manteau*
2. *un fez*
3. *un tas*
4. *le cheval*
5. *le cheveu*

Chapter 3

Practice 3.1

Give the English equivalent of the French, then the French equivalent of the English:

Example: *un chanteur* ⇒ a singer, an apartment ⇒ *un appartement*.

1. *un artiste*
2. *une secrétaire*
3. *des assistants*
4. a village
5. a house
6. (some) towns

Practice 3.2

Give the English equivalent of the French, then the French equivalent of the English:

Example: *le chanteur* ⇒ the singer, the apartment ⇒ *l'appartement*.

1. *le pied*
2. *la main*
3. *l'oreille*
4. *les yeux*
5. the blouse
6. the shirt
7. the anorak
8. the shoes

Chapter 4

Practice 4.1
Make these masculine adjectives feminine:

Example: *un grand artichaut – une ...... aubergine ⇒ – une grande aubergine*

1. *un concombre vert – une salade ......*
2. *un citron jaune – une banane ......*
3. *un mauvais champignon – une ...... pomme*
4. *un abricot mûr – une pêche ......*

Practice 4.2
Make these singular phrases plural:

Example: *un cheval français ⇒ des chevaux français*

1. *un cochon rose*
2. *une vache brune*
3. *le chien méchant*
4. *la souris timide*
5. *un animal domestique*

Practice 4.3
Write the following in French:

Example: my mother ⇒ *ma mère*

1. my sister
2. my cousin Pierre
3. my friends
4. my sisters
5. my friend Henri
6. my dress

Practice 4.4
Write the following in French:

Example: your aunt ⇒ *ta tante*

1. your uncle
2. your parents
3. your television
4. your suit*
5. your cousin Angélique
6. your brothers

  * *le costume* = the (man's) suit; *le tailleur* = the (woman's) suit

Practice 4.5
Write the following in French:

Example: his book ⇒ *son livre*

1. his car
2. her car
3. his friend
4. his friends
5. her bones*
6. its bones

un os = a bone

Practice 4.6

Choose the correct possessive adjectives to complete this story. Then turn the story into English:

Example: *Je suis dans (mon / ma / mes) lit.* ⇒ *Je suis dans **mon** lit. I am in my bed.*

(Mon / Ma / Mes) chien Bruno entre dans (sa / ta / ma) chambre. Il veut (ses / sa / son) petit déjeuner. Je mets (tes / mes / ses) lunettes et je regarde (ton / son / mon) réveil: 5 heures!
'Bruno! Retourne dans (ton / ta / tes) lit! (Mes / Sa / Ton) petit déjeuner est à 7 heures 30, et après, c'est (ta / ses / mon) promenade. (Ses / Mes / Tes) amis sont là, dans le parc, surtout (tes / ton / ta) petite amie Brunette. Tu es content?'
Et Bruno agite (sa / ses / son) queue!

Chapter 5

Practice 5.1

Write the appropriate French pronoun (*je, tu, il, elle, on, nous, vous, ils, elles*) before the following verbs: In some cases there will be more than one correct answer.

Example: *… mangez* ⇒ *vous mangez*

1. *… aime*
2. *… parles*
3. *… regarde*
4. *… écoutez*
5. *… cherchent*
6. *… jouons*

Practice 5.2

Add the appropriate endings to the following verbs and then write their English meaning:

Example: *tu (manger)* ⇒ *tu manges* = you eat / you are eating

1. *je (jouer)*
2. *nous (regarder)*
3. *elles (écouter)*
4. *tu (chercher)*
5. *vous (aimer)*
6. *ils (parler)*

Practice 5.3

Write the correct form of *être* to go with the following pronouns and then give the English meaning:

Example: *je ….* ⇒ *je suis = I am*

1. *on …*
2. *vous …*
3. *tu …*
4. *elle …*
5. *nous …*
6. *ils …*

Practice 5.4

Write the correct form of *avoir* to go with the following nouns or pronouns and then give the English meaning:

Example: *Pauline …* ⇒ *Pauline a = Pauline has*

1. *tu …*
2. *les amis …*
3. *on …*
4. *nous …*
5. *vous …*
6. *j' …*
7. *Frank … froid*
8. *mes parents … raison*
9. *j' … faim*
10. *mon frère … vingt ans*

Practice 5.5

Write the correct form of *aller* to go with the following nouns or pronouns and then give the English meaning:

Example: *nous ... ⇒ nous allons* = we go

1. *Loïc ...*
2. *vous ...*
3. *je ...*

4. *mes cousines ...*
5. *tu ...*
6. *on ...*

Practice 5.6

Write the correct form of *faire* to go with the following nouns or pronouns and then give the English meaning:

Example: *tu ... ⇒ tu fais* = you do / make

1. *on ......*
2. *mon copain et moi ......*
3. *je ......*

4. *vous ......*
5. *son chien ......*
6. *ses chats ......*

Practice 5.7

Write the correct form of *prendre* to go with the following nouns or pronouns and then give the English meaning:

Example: *vous ...... ⇒ vous prenez* = you take

1. *on ......*
2. *tu ......*
3. *je ......*
4. *nous ......*
5. *Esther et Céline ......*
6. *ton oncle ......*

Practice 5.8

Complete the following sentences with the correct form of *être* = 'to be', *avoir* = 'to have', *aller* = 'to go', *faire* = 'to do' or *prendre* = 'to take'. Then give the English meaning:

Example: *Je ...... des achats (faire) ⇒ Je fais des achats* = I do the shopping (I go shopping).

1. *Le bébé ...... trois dents. (avoir)*
2. *Nous ...... au cinéma en voiture. (aller)*
3. *Je ...... fatigué. (être)*
4. *Marie ...... seize ans. (avoir)*
5. *Il ...... chaud (faire), donc il ...... chaud. (avoir)*

6. *Tu ...... le train ou l'avion? (prendre)*
7. *Elles ...... en autobus. (aller)*
8. *On ...... un café? (prendre)*
9. *Vous ...... américain? (être)*
10. *Les garçons ...... de la natation. (faire)*

Practice 5.9

Translate into French:

Example: Take an umbrella! (formal) ⇒ *Prenez un parapluie!*

1. Let's play tennis!
2. Listen to the CD! (familiar singular)
3. Stay here! (plural)

4. Look at the photos! (familiar singular)
5. Let's go to Paris!
6. Make an omelette! (formal)

Chapter 6

Practice 6.1

Complete the following, using the phrases in brackets, to make the sentence future and then give the English meaning:

Example: *Demain, je ... (voir mes amis).* ⇒ *Demain je vais voir mes amis* = 'Tomorrow I'm going to see my friends'.

1. *Demain, Marie ...... (partir en voyage).*
2. *Nous ...... (acheter des CD).*
3. *Tu ...... (faire du ski).*
4. *Vous ...... (écrire un mail).*
5. *On ...... (regarder un DVD).*
6. *Eric...... (jouer au football).*
7. *Michel et Caroline ... (aller au restaurant).*

Practice 6.2

Read what these people are doing today, then write what they are going to do tomorrow, using the phrases in brackets:

Example: *Aujourd'hui, tu manges à la maison, et demain?* ⇒ *Demain je vais manger au restaurant.*

1. *Aujourd'hui, Karim fait du vélo, et demain? (faire du ski nautique)*
2. *Aujourd'hui, ma mère achète un livre de cuisine, et demain? (préparer des crêpes)*
3. *Aujourd'hui, mes cousins jouent au tennis, et demain? (jouer au golf)*
4. *Aujourd'hui, vous allez au concert, et demain? (aller au match)*
5. *Aujourd'hui, on commence le livre 'Harry Potter', et demain? (finir le livre)*

Chapter 7

Practice 7.1

Read these words aloud, and add the acute accents where appropriate:

Example: *mechant* ⇒ *méchant*

1. *decider, je decide, elle a decide*
2. *cinema*
3. *repetition*
4. *Celine*
5. *tu as ecoute, il ecoute, vous ecoutez*

Practice 7.2

Read these words aloud, and add the grave accents where appropriate:

Example: *pere* ⇒ *père*

1. *elle achete*
2. *Hélene*
3. *tu répetes*
4. *frere*
5. *regle*
6. *vous appelez*
7. *nous achetons*
8. *on jette*

Practice 7.3

Read these words aloud, and add the circumflex accents on the words in French where appropriate:

Example: *bete* = beast ⇒ '*bête*'

1. *fete* = feast
2. *arreter* = arrest
3. *honnete* = honest
4. *quete* = quest
5. *pates* = pasta

Practice 7.4
Add the circumflex accents on the French words where appropriate:

Example: *hote* = host ⇒ *hôte*

1.   *platre* = plaster
2.   *couter* = to cost
3.   *mat* = mast
4.   *aout* = August
5.   *maitre* = master

Practice 7.5
Try and work out the English meanings of these French words, remembering that the circumflex accent often replaces a missing 's':

Example: *hôtel* = hostel

1.   *hâte*
2.   *pâté*
3.   *tâche*
4.   *rôti*
5.   *croûte*

Chapter 8

Practice 8.1
Give the correct form of *avoir* to complete these sentences in the perfect tense and then give the English meaning:

Example: *J'...... travaillé jusqu'à cinq heures.* ⇒ *J'ai travaillé jusqu'à cinq heures* = I worked until five o'clock.

1.   *Nous ...... regardé la télé.*
2.   *Il ...... parlé avec ses amis.*
3.   *Les filles ...... adoré le concert.*
4.   *Tu ...... aimé le film?*
5.   *Vous ...... déjà mangé?*

Practice 8.2
Indicate whether the following sentences are present (pres.) or past (perf.):

Example: *Le film a commencé à 21 heures* ⇒ **perf.**

1.   *Je préfère la limonade au lait.*
2.   *Michel a donné un cadeau à son amie.*
3.   *Nous avons nagé dans la mer.*
4.   *Vous avez trouvé vos lunettes?*
5.   *Où est-ce que tu habites?*
6.   *Tu restes dans un hôtel?*
7.   *Je pense, donc je suis ... fatigué.*
8.   *Elle a oublié son billet.*
9.   *Ils ont refusé de partir.*
10.   *Il a répété la question trois fois.*

Practice 8.3
Write what these people did or took, using the phrases in brackets:

Example: *Julien ... (faire du ski).* ⇒ *Julien a fait du ski.*

1.   *Marie-Ange ... (prendre un sac à dos).*
2.   *Nadine et Aïsha ... (faire les courses).*
3.   *Vous ... (faire du vélo).*
4.   *Je ... (prendre le train).*
5.   *Sylvie et moi ... (faire de l'équitation).*
6.   *On ... (prendre un café).*
7.   *Elle ... (prendre son temps).*
8.   *Tu as ... (faire la cuisine).*

Practice 8.4

Write where these people went, using the phrases in the brackets:

Example: *Les filles … (aller aux magasins).* ⇒ *Les filles sont allées aux magasins.*

1. *Jean … (aller en ville).*
2. *Nous … (aller au gymnase).*
3. *Alain et toi, vous … (aller en Belgique)?*
4. *On … (aller au parc).*
5. *Tu … (aller à la piscine).*
6. *Je … (aller à Genève).*

Practice 8.5

Send an e-mail to a friend to tell him about meeting your favourite singer. You will need to use forms of *être* and *avoir* to describe what he was like and what he had.

Example: *Il …… les yeux violets.* ⇒ *Il avait les yeux violets.*

1. *Il …… les cheveux roux.*
2. *Il …… vachement beau.*
3. *Il …… environ 30 ans.* (remember, you 'have years' in French!)
4. *Moi, j' …… complètement excité(e).*
5. *J' …… des difficultés à parler.*
6. *Il …… un pantalon très chic.*
7. *Ses chaussures …… des lacets roses.*
8. *Il …… vraiment sympa.*
9. *Ses chansons …… super cool.*
10. *Il y …… énormément de fans au concert.*

Practice 8.6

Change this story from the present tense to the past. Then write the story in English:

Example: *J'ai un jour de vacances* ⇒ *J'avais un jour de vacances* = I had a day off.

Je <u>vais</u> à la plage. Je <u>retrouve</u> mes copains. Nous <u>jouons</u> au volley. Puis nous <u>décidons</u> de nager dans la mer. L'eau <u>est</u> froide. Je <u>passe</u> une bonne journée et je <u>suis</u> bien content(e).

Practice 8.7

Show which tense is being used: past (perf.), present (pres.) or future (fut.):

Example: *Jean est allé au marché* ⇒ perf.

1. *Les joueurs de foot arrivent au stade.*
2. *Vous allez acheter des glaces.*
3. *Tu aimes le poulet?*
4. *Elle a changé de place.*
5. *Nous sommes allés en Suisse.*
6. *Patrick va partir à 8 heures.*
7. *Il a une nouvelle moto.*
8. *Ils sont très grands.*
9. *Vous avez acheté beaucoup de choses?*
10. *Je vais au match de tennis.*

Practice 8.8

Match up the French and English phrases. Then complete the sentences below, changing the tense as appropriate:

Example: 1. *actuellement*   (h) at the moment
             3. *demain*   (c) tomorrow

Actuellement je suis au bord de la mer, mais dans dix jours je ...... en montagne. ⇒ *Actuellement je suis au bord de la mer, mais dans dix jours je* **vais être** *en montagne.*

1.	*actuellement*	(a) yesterday
2.	*aujourd'hui*	(b) in ten days' time
3.	*demain*	(c) tomorrow
4.	*dans dix jours*	(d) the day after tomorrow
5.	*maintenant*	(e) last week
6.	*il y a trois jours*	(f) next year
7.	*hier*	(g) now
8.	*l'année prochaine*	(h) at the moment
9.	*après-demain*	(i) today
10.	*la semaine dernière*	(j) three days ago

1. *Aujourd'hui je mange à la maison, mais hier j' ...... au restaurant.*
2. *La semaine dernière, il est allé à Londres, mais après-demain il ...... à Glasgow.*
3. *L'année prochaine, nous allons visiter le Maroc, mais maintenant nous ...... la Tunisie.*
4. *Il y a trois jours, elles ont acheté des vêtements, mais demain elles ...... des chaussures.*

Chapter 9

Practice 9.1

Change these statements into questions. Say them aloud (remembering to raise your voice at the end):

Example: *Il pleut.* ⇒ *Est-ce qu'il pleut?*

1. *Elle est allée à la gare.*
2. *Vous avez déjà visité Bruxelles.*
3. *Ils vont acheter une grande voiture.*
4. *Emmanuelle va partir bientôt.*
5. *Les Français mangent des escargots.*

Practice 9.2

Complete the following questions by choosing the most suitable question word(s), then give the English meaning:

Example: *...... est-ce que tu es allé?* ⇒ **Où** *est-ce que tu es allé?* = Where did you go?

1. *Avec ...... est-ce que tu es allé?*
2. *...... est-ce que tu aimes la France?*
3. *...... est-ce que tu vas en vacances? La semaine prochaine?*
4. *...... est-ce que le film a duré?*
5. *...... est-ce que tu as fait le trajet? En avion?*
6. *...... est-ce que tu as fait hier soir?*
7. *...... est-ce que tu as payé cette robe? Plus de 100€?*
8. *...... chemisier est-ce que tu préfères?*
9. *A ...... heure est-ce que tu es allé au match?*
10. *Est-ce que tu sais ...... il est allé?*

Chapter 10

Practice 10.1

Make the following statements negative:

Example: *Je vends ma maison* ⇒ *Je **ne** vends **pas** ma maison.*

1. *Pierre est petit.*
2. *Elles écoutent la musique.*
3. *Nous regardons les DVD.*
4. *Tu vas au cinéma?*
5. *Vous aimez le fromage?*

Practice 10.2

Make the following statements negative:

Example: *J'ai parlé avec ma voisine.* ⇒ *Je **n'**ai **pas** parlé avec ma voisine.*

1. *On est allé à la pâtisserie.*
2. *Les Anglais ont aimé les cuisses de grenouille.*
3. *Elles ont acheté la plus belle boîte de chocolats.*
4. *Edith a chanté sa dernière chanson.*
5. *Il a fait froid.*

Chapter 11

Practice 11.1

Fill in the gaps in the story with the correct prepositions (*à, au, à la, à l', aux, en*). Then give the English meaning:

Example: *L'année dernière je suis allé ...... Montréal.* ⇒ *L'année dernière je suis allé **à** Montréal.* = Last year I went to Montreal.

C'était ma première visite ...... Canada. D'habitude, je passe mes vacances ...... France, ... Bordeaux, ou ...... Espagne, et une fois je suis allé ...... Etats-Unis. ...... aéroport, j'ai montré mon passeport ...... douanier. Je suis très vite arrivé ...... mon hôtel en taxi, parce que le chauffeur ne s'est pas arrêté ...... feux!

Practice 11.2

Fill in the gaps in the story with the correct preposition (*de, d', du, de la, de l', des*). Then give the English meaning:

Example: *A la réception, on m'a donné la clé ...... ma chambre.* ⇒ *A la réception, on m'a donné la clé **de** ma chambre.* = At reception, I was given my room key (literally: the key of my room).

Plus tard, je suis sorti ...... hôtel pour visiter les attractions ...... ville. J'ai consulté l'horaire ...... autobus. Il y en avait un qui partait ...... coin ...... rue. J'ai vu beaucoup ...... gens qui rentraient ...... bureau ou qui regardaient les vitrines ...... magasins ...... centre. Près ...... gare, il y avait un petit parc ...... attractions.

Practice 11.3

Write these in French..

Example: my mother's cat ⇒ *le chat de ma mère*

1. the lady's garden
2. the doctor's house
3. my sister's birthday
4. the student's books
5. the students' books

Practice 11.4

Here is the recipe for a pizza you want to make for your French host family. Ask if they have these ingredients.

Example: *farine* ⇒ *Est-ce que vous avez de la farine?*

Ingrédients
(feminine)	(masculine)
farine	*fromage* ✗
tomates ✗	*anchois* ✗
purée de tomates ✗	*sel et poivre*
huile	
olives	

Practice 11.5

Looking back at Practice 11-4, write which four items the French family don't have (the ones marked with a ✗, using a negative sentence.

Example: *tomates* ⇒ *Vous n'avez pas **de** tomates.*

Practice 11.6

Choose the correct preposition to complete each sentence. Then give the English meaning:

Example: *Je suis allé (chez / de / entre) elle* ⇒ *Je suis allé **chez** elle* = I went to her house.

1. *Paris est (en / dans / à) France.*
2. *Nous allons prendre le tunnel (sur / sous / jusqu'à) la Manche.*
3. *Mon frère est parti (pour / en / sans) moi.*
4. *Elle est rentrée (devant / avant / jusqu'à) dix heures.*
5. *Mes amis ont acheté un appartement (dans / en / à) Glasgow.*
6. *Marie va en vacances (avec / derrière / entre) ses parents.*
7. *Le cinéma est (jusqu'à / pour / entre) le restaurant et le complexe multisports.*
8. *(Devant / Avant / Entre) le déjeuner, il a téléphoné (avec / pour / à) son copain.*

Practice 11.7

Complete each of these sentences, using *pour, pendant* or *depuis,* as appropriate. Then give the English meaning:

Example: *Nous regardons le match ...... un quart d'heure.* ⇒ *Nous regardons le match **depuis** un quart d'heure* = We have been watching the match for a quarter of an hour.

1. *La semaine prochaine, nous allons partir en France ...... trois jours.*
2. *Mes cousins sont restés chez moi ...... une semaine.*
3. *Elle habite ici ...... cinq ans.*
4. *J'ai habité à Paris ...... deux ans.*
5. *Le footballeur ne va pas jouer ...... huit mois.*

Chapter 12

Practice 12.1

Replace the underlined subject nouns by subject pronouns. Then give the English meaning:

Example: *Elodie a un chat.* ⇒ ***Elle** a un chat.* = She has a cat.

1. *Le chat s'appelle Minou.*
2. *Minou aime les oiseaux.*
3. *Les oiseaux habitent dans une cage.*
4. *La cage est blanche et bleue.*
5. *Le père d'Elodie a acheté la cage.*

Practice 12.2

Are the words underlined subject (s) or object (o)?

Example: <u>Je</u> regarde <u>le film</u>. ⇒ 'Je (s); le film (o).

1. <u>Marie</u> a acheté <u>des provisions</u>.
2. Où est <u>le gâteau</u> qu'<u>elle</u> a acheté?
3. <u>La police</u> a arrêté <u>le criminel</u>.
4. <u>Le livre</u> que <u>je</u> lis est intéressant.
5. Quand est-ce que <u>tu</u> as regardé <u>le match</u>?

Practice 12.3

Replace the underlined object nouns by object pronouns. Then write the meaning in English:

Example: Je regarde <u>mon chien</u>. ⇒ Je **le** regarde. = I look at him.

1. Il mange <u>les os</u>. ⇒ Il ...... mange.
2. Nous regardons <u>le</u> DVD. ⇒ Nous ...... regardons.
3. Mon frère a acheté <u>le nouveau CD des Rolling Bones</u>. ⇒ Mon frère ...... a acheté.
4. Il va lire <u>le livre</u> très vite. ⇒ Il va ...... lire très vite.
5. Moi, je préfère <u>les magazines</u>. ⇒ Moi, je ...... préfère.

Practice 12.4

Unjumble the French sentences to go with their English equivalent:

Example: We bought it – acheté Nous avons l'. ⇒ We bought it = Nous l'avons acheté.

1. I often see him. – Je vois le souvent.
2. His mother sells them. – mère Sa vend les.
3. The telly? They watch it a lot. – beaucoup la La regardent télé Ils?.
4. The ticket? He paid for it at the counter. – billet l' payé a au il guichet le?.
5. Whisky? She does not drink it. – Le le boit whisky Elle ne pas?.

Chapter 13

Practice 13.1

Read these aloud and add a cedilla where necessary to produce the right pronunciation of 'c':

Example: Francoise ⇒ Fran**ç**oise.

1. une casserole
2. des haricots
3. une lecon
4. elle commence
5. ca casse
6. les Francais
7. vous menacez
8. nous commencons

Practice 13.2

Read these aloud and add a tréma where necessary to isolate a vowel sound:

Example: les Caraibes ⇒ les Caraïbes.

1. Noel
2. la maison
3. Anais Anais
4. Joelle
5. une moitié
6. la moelle

Practice 13.3

Your friend does not know how to get accents, cedillas and trémas on his word processor. Help him finish his e-mail before he sends it:

Example: Salut! Enfin la liberte! ⇒ Salut! Enfin la liberté!

Les examens sont termines et je peux passer la fete de Noel avec mon frere et sa fiancee. Programme d'activites: cine, disco, arrivee de son corres francais, Gael. Une bonne facon de se detendre!

Chapter 14

Practice 14.1

In this list of masculine nouns, most are easy to identify as masculine. Show which ones by marking them with a tick (√). Mark those that are not easy to identify with a question mark:

Example: *journal* √ – *magazine* ?

1.	*masque*	7.	*crabe*
2.	*voisin*	8.	*bus*
3.	*programme*	9.	*mètre*
4.	*astrologue*	10.	*paravent*
5.	*Japon*	11.	*manteau*
6.	*privilège*	12.	*alibi*

Practice 14.2

In this list of feminine nouns, most are easy to identify as feminine. Show which ones by marking them with a tick (√). Mark those that are not easy to identify with a question mark:

Example: *girafe* ? – *voiture* √

1.	*inscription*	7.	*Afrique*
2.	*bouche*	8.	*statue*
3.	*plante*	9.	*chatte*
4.	*rage*	10.	*couverture*
5.	*journée*	11.	*chambre*
6.	*distance*	12.	*essence*

Practice 14.3

Try to help this French person who has used a dictionary to write this note. Clearly he has had problems with words that have a different meaning in the masculine and feminine.

Example: After my sum = After my nap

After my sum I looked at the first pageboy of my pound of kitchen. I found a recipe for cake tins, prepared in the froth mode.

Practice 14.4

Choose the correct word from those in brackets, by checking whether the relevant underlined noun or pronoun is masculine or feminine:

Example: *(Mon / Ma)* <u>samedi</u> *(idéal / idéale)* ⇒ **Mon** samedi **idéal**

Pour commencer je fais (le / la) grasse <u>matinée</u> jusqu'à dix <u>heures</u> et (demi / demie). Après (le / la) (petit / petite) <u>déjeuner</u>, je prends (le / la) <u>bus</u> pour aller (au / à la) <u>piscine</u>. Je fais (du / de la) <u>natation</u> jusqu'à <u>midi</u> et (demi / demie) avec (un / une) très (joli / jolie) <u>fille</u>. Puis je retrouve (mon / ma) <u>copine</u>, et nous allons prendre (un / une) <u>verre</u> ensemble. Plus tard je mange (un / une) <u>sandwich</u> avec (mon / ma) <u>fiancée</u>, et je (le / la) laisse pour aller regarder (un / une) <u>film</u> avec (le / la) (petit / petite) <u>amie</u> de (mon / ma) <u>voisin</u>. C'est (un / une) <u>personne</u> très (séduisant / séduisante), pour qui j'ai (un / une) (grand / grande) <u>amitié</u>. Ensuite, je prends (le / la) <u>dîner</u> chez (le / la) <u>cousine</u> de (mon / ma) <u>mère</u>. <u>Elle</u> est (mûr / mûre) et toujours (charmant / charmante). Finalement je rentre chez moi et je passe (le / la) <u>soirée</u> avec (mon / ma) <u>femme</u>. (Un / Une) <u>journée</u> bien (intéressant / intéressante)!

Chapter 15

Practice 15.1

You have just returned from a holiday in Spain. Your best friend wants to hear all about it. Answer her questions, following the prompts in English. Take care to place the adjectives after their nouns:

Example: – *'Tu as passé une bonne semaine?'* – No, I had a horrible week. *(semaine – horrible)* ⇒ *'Non, j'ai passé une semaine horrible.'*

1. *Comment était l'hôtel?* – 'It was a comfortable hotel.' (*hôtel – confortable*)
2. *C'était bien équipé?* – 'It was OK, there was an enormous swimming pool.' (*piscine – énorme*)
3. *Donc la piscine était bien?* – 'No, because I don't like cold water!' (*eau – froide*)
4. *Vous avez bien mangé?* – 'No, I hate Spanish food!' (*nourriture – espagnole*)
5. *Mais les garçons espagnols sont sympa, n'est-ce pas?* – 'I don't know, I only spoke with English boys.' (*garçons – anglais*)
6. *Tu vas y retourner l'été prochain?* 'No, next summer I would like to go to an interesting country.' (*pays – intéressant*)

Practice 15.2

A French friend is showing you photos of his pets. What does he say to describe them? (Use the key words suggested). Take care: some adjectives will go before, others after the noun.

Example: *Minet* – cat – small – white. ⇒ *Voici Minet, c'est mon petit chat blanc.*

1. *Médor* – dog – big – brown
2. *Zigzag* – snake – long – yellow
3. *Jeannot* – rabbit – tall – black
4. *Bulle* – fish – old – gold / red
5. *Roland* – rat – beautiful – friendly
6. *Sacha* – cat – other – brightly coloured*

*brightly coloured = *chamarré*

Practice 15.3

Give the English for these phrases:

Example: *un sport cher* = an expensive sport

1. *ses chaussettes propres*
2. *ses propres chaussettes*
3. *un ancien palais*
4. *sa chère tante*
5. *son seul jour de vacances*

Practice 15.4

Turn these phrases into French, taking care where you place the adjectives:

Example: a big flat ⇒ *un grand appartement*

1. last Monday
2. a peaceful village
3. a bad meal
4. a young singer
5. the poor dog
6. the tall building
7. my little brother
8. his black cat
9. the only taxi
10. your own flat

Practice 15.5

Choose from the list below the most appropriate adjective for each noun, taking care to select its correct spelling:

Example: *des bananes ... ⇒ des bananes jaunes*

1. *les monuments ...*
2. *les ... enfants*
3. *la cuisine ...*
4. *les matchs ...*
5. *la semaine ...*
6. *une chatte ...*
7. *des appartements ...*
8. *un ... repas*

noir / noire	*historique / historiques*	*jaune / jaunes*
prochaine / prochaines	*régional / régionale*	*jeune / jeunes*
grand / grands	*passionnants / passionnantes*	*cher / chers*

Practice 15.6

Choose the most appropriate nouns from the list below to fill the gaps in this story. Check the adjective endings carefully before you make your choice:

Example: *La ...... dernière, c'était l'anniversaire de mon copain. ⇒ La **semaine** dernière, c'était l'anniversaire de mon copain.*

Il a organisé une grande ......, avec beaucoup de ...... moderne et un énorme ...... avec une belle ...... Je portais mon ...... neuf et mes ...... blanches. Comme cadeau, j'ai acheté un nouveau ...... et une jolie .... Nous avons fait un grand ......, et la vieille ......, qui n'est pas une ...... gentille, nous a dit d'arrêter notre bonne ...... Quel ...... !

dommage	fête	gâteau	personne	voisine
jean	carte	baskets	décoration	~~semaine~~
musique	CD	soirée	bruit	

Practice 15.7

Write the correct form of the adjectives to go with the nouns, taking care with their position:

Example: *une voiture* (new) = *une **nouvelle** voiture*

1. *une journée* (beautiful)
2. *un endroit* (beautiful)
3. *un château* (beautiful)
4. *le grand-père* (old)
5. *la maison* (old)
6. *les grands-parents* (old)
7. *l'homme* (old)
8. *l'horaire* (new)
9. *l'élève* (f.) (new)
10. *un film* (new)

Practice 15.8

Using the adjectives from the list below, compare Noah's elephant and mosquito. Write two sentences with *plus ...... que*, two with '*moins ...... que*', two with '*(aus)si ...... que*', and one with the special form for '*bon*':

Example: *Les éléphants sont **moins petits que** les moustiques.*

petit	utile	stupide	léger	grand	énervant	féroce	bon

Practice 15.9

Noah is examing the animals in his Ark. Correct what he says about the elephant and the mosquito in relation to the rest of the animals (all his statements need correcting):

Example: *Le moustique est l'animal le plus lourd. ⇒ Non, le moustique est l'animal **le moins lourd**.*

1. *L'éléphant est l'animal le plus petit.*
2. *Le moustique est l'insecte le plus agréable.*
3. *L'éléphant est la créature la moins patiente.*
4. *Le moustique est la créature la plus grande.*
5. *L'éléphant est la bête la moins bizarre.*
6. *L'éléphant est le moins bon pour travailler.*

Chapter 16

Practice 16.1

Choose the appropriate demonstrative adjective:

Example: *(Cet / Ce) soir, je ne vais pas rester chez moi.* ⇒ **Ce** *soir, je ne vais pas rester chez moi.*

Toute (cette / ces) semaine j'ai beaucoup travaillé. Pour (cet / cette) raison, j'ai décidé d'aller au centre de loisirs. A (ces / cet) endroit on peut choisir toutes sortes d'activités. (Ce / Ces) possibilités permettent de bien apprécier (ce / cet) complexe multisports.

Practice 16.2

Complete the following dialogue with the appropriate French words for 'my', 'your', 'his', 'her' and 'its'. Choose the most obvious answer each time:

Example: *Sylvain: Est-ce que tu es sorti avec ...... copains?* ⇒ *Est-ce que tu es sorti avec **tes** copains?*

Fabien:	*Oui, avec ...... copains et ...... frère.*
Sylvain:	*Et ...... frère, il a pris ...... propre voiture?*
Fabien:	*Non, il a pris la voiture de ...... mère.*
Sylvain:	*Tu es allé à ...... club préféré?*
Fabien:	*Oui, et il y avait ...... chanteuse favorite, accompagnée de ...... groupe.*

Practice 16.3

Write these in French:

Example: your scarf = *ton_écharpe*

1. his anorak
2. her anorak
3. your friend Mustapha
4. your friend Fatima
5. her friends
6. its eyes
7. its nose
8. my brothers and my sisters

Practice 16.4

Write these in French:

Example: our house = *notre maison*

1. our lounge
2. our bedrooms
3. our garden
4. our kitchen
5. our garages

Practice 16.5

Write these in French:

Example: your holidays = *vos vacances*

1. your hotel
2. your flight
3. your activities
4. your pool
5. your passports

Practice 16.6
Write these in French:

Example: their family = *leur famille*

1. their parents
2. their mother
3. their sister
4. their cousins
5. their uncle

Practice 16.7
Reassure this lady that you understand what she is saying to you. You will need to change 'I' and 'my' into 'you' and 'your', etc.

Example: *J'ai perdu mon sac …* ⇒ Ah, bon? **Vous** avez perdu **votre** sac?

Dedans, il y a mon porte-monnaie …
Et aussi, ma carte d'identité …
Et puis, une photo de mes chats …
Egalement, mes cachets d'aspirine …
Et enfin, mon carnet d'adresses …

Practice 16.8
You have seen the notice shown below. As you think your French friend will be interested, you call her to tell her about it. You will need to change from the formal '*vous*', '*votre*', '*vos*', to the familiar '*tu*', '*ton*', '*ta*', '*tes*'.

Example: *Pour vos loisirs d'été* ⇒ Pour **tes** loisirs d'été

> *Tout pour vos loisirs d'été,*
> *Tout pour votre sport favori!*
> *Votre équipement,*
> *vos cours avec moniteurs,*
> *votre assurance, votre carte info –*
> *Achetez ici votre billet:*
> *50€ seulement.*

Chapter 17

Practice 17.1
Change these adjectives into adverbs, say them, and give the English meaning:

Example: *facile* ⇒ **facilement** = easily

1. *calme*
2. *réel*
3. *traditionnel*
4. *constant*
5. *heureux*

Practice 17.2

Complete these sentences with a suitable adverb (they do not all end in **-ment**!). Then give the English meaning:

> **Example**: *Il trouve ça <u>normal</u>, tout a fonctionné......* ⇒ *Il trouve ça <u>normal</u>, tout a fonctionné* **normalement**. = He finds it normal, it all worked normally.

1. *C'est un train <u>rapide</u>, il voyage ....*
2. *Le repas était <u>bon</u>, nous avons ...... mangé.*
3. *Cette histoire est <u>récente</u>, c'est arrivé ....*
4. *Le service est <u>régulier</u>, les bus arrivent ....*
5. *Les enfants sont <u>gentils</u>, ils jouent ....*
6. *Je suis malade, je ne vais pas ....*
7. *Avec ce médicament, je vais aller ....*
8. *C'est ...... le train pour le Stade de France, n'est-ce pas?*
9. *Il y a eu un accident <u>tragique</u>, l'assistante du magicien est morte ....*

Chapter 18

Practice 18.1

Give the correct form of these reflexive verbs, then give the English meaning:

> **Example**: *tu (se lever)* ⇒ *tu te lèves* = you get up

1. *elle (s'amuser)*
2. *vous (s'habiller)*
3. *je (se reposer)*
4. *ils (se raser)*
5. *nous (se dépêcher)*
6. *on (se doucher)*

Practice 18.2

Make up sentences to explain what Béa the babysitter has to do, for herself and for the baby:

> **Example**: *Béa* **se réveille**, *puis elle* **réveille** *le bébé.*

1. *(se) lever ......*
2. *(se) laver ......*
3. *(s') habiller ......*
4. *(se) promener ......*
5. *(se) changer ......*
6. *(se) coucher ......*

Practice 18.3

Simplify the following sentences, using reflexive verbs:

> **Example**: *Lisa parle à Denise et Denise parle à Lisa.* ⇒ *Lisa et Denise* **se parlent**.

1. *Le chat regarde l'oiseau et l'oiseau regarde le chat.*
2. *Myriam voit Philippe et Philippe voit Myriam sur leurs portables.*
3. *David envoie un mail à Claire et Claire envoie un mail à David.*
4. *Le 1er janvier, les gens disent: 'Bonne année!' aux autres gens, et vice versa.*
5. *Mark écrit une carte à Linda et Linda écrit une carte à Mark.*

Chapter 19

Practice 19.1

Write the correct form of the following –ir verbs:

> **Example**: *partir – nous* ⇒ *nous* **partons**

1. *finir – on ......*
2. *grandir – Suzanne ......*
3. *sortir – les jeunes ......*
4. *dormir – Ali et Khaled ......*
5. *grossir – tu ......*
6. *verdir – le jardin ......*
7. *vieillir – je ......*
8. *jaunir – les plantes ......*

Practice 19.2

Match the two halves, then give the English meaning:

Example: *tu – viens* ⇒ *tu viens* = you come

1.	*je*	(a)	*tient*
2.	*elles*	(b)	*viennent*
3.	*il*	(c)	*venons*
4.	*nous*	(d)	*tiens*
5.	*vous*	(e)	*tenez*

Practice 19.3

Choose the correct pronoun(s) to go with the verb, then give the English meaning:

Example: *(je / vous / tu) dois* ⇒ *je / tu dois* = I / you have to

1. *(ils / il / on) sait*
2. *(vous / tu / on) devez*
3. *(vous / nous / elles) savons*
4. *(je / elle / ils) doivent*
5. *(nous / tu / vous) savez*

Practice 19.4

Choose the correct verb form, and give the English meaning:

Example: *tu (peut / peux)* ⇒ *tu **peux*** = you are able to / can.

1. *elle (veulent / veut)*
2. *vous (voulez / veulent)*
3. *je (peut / peux)*
4. *on (voulons / veut)*
5. *ils (peut / peuvent)*

Practice 19.5

Make these verbs plural and give the English meaning:

Example: *elle ouvre* ⇒ *elles ouvrent* = they open.

1. *il offre*
2. *tu offres*
3. *j'ouvre*
4. *il ouvre*
5. *elle offre*

Practice 19.6

Complete the endings of these regular –re verbs, then give the English meaning:

Example: *Mes parents attend......* ⇒ *Mes parents attend**ent*** = My parents are waiting.

1. *Vous entend...... le bébé qui pleure?*
2. *Loïc descend...... du train.*
3. *Ici on vend...... toutes sortes de souvenirs.*
4. *Les stars répond...... aux questions de l'interviewer.*
5. *Nous t'attend...... devant la gare.*
6. *Je n'entend...... pas bien la musique sur mon lecteur CD.*
7. *Tu vend...... ta voiture?*
8. *Ma copine descend...... la piste de ski à toute vitesse.*

Practice 19.7

In this mobile telephone conversation, Axelle and Salomé are arranging to go out. Unfortunately the reception is poor, and the verbs 'être', 'faire' and 'prendre' are missing! Put them back:

Example: *Axelle: 'Qu'est-ce que tu ...... ?'* ⇒ *'Qu'est-ce que tu **fais**?'*

Axelle:	*Où ...... tu?*
Salomé:	*Je ...... au supermarché, et toi?*
Axelle:	*Moi, je ...... le petit déjeuner.*
Salomé:	*Tu veux ...... un pique-nique cet après-midi?*
Axelle:	*Pourquoi pas? Il ...... beau.*
Salomé:	*D'accord. Je viens te ...... chez toi à onze heures.*

Practice 19.8

Complete the following sentences with forms of '*boire*' and '*dire*'. Then give the English meaning:

Example: *Je ...... un coca.* ⇒ *Je **bois** un coca.* = I drink a coke.

1. *Elle ...... qu'elle est fatiguée.*
2. *Tu ...... qu'il m'aime?*
3. *Mon père ...... trop de bière.*
4. *Qu'est-ce que vous ......? Parlez plus fort!*
5. *On ...... que la grammaire française est difficile.*
6. *Nous ne ...... pas d'alcool.*

Chapter 20

Practice 20.1

Read what is happening today, and explain that the same thing will happen tomorrow. Then write the English meaning:

Example: *Aujourd'hui je ne travaille pas et demain je ......* ⇒ *je ne **travaillerai** pas.* = I shall not work.

1. *Ce matin je joue au tennis, et demain matin aussi je ......*
2. *Aujourd'hui à midi on mange une pizza, et demain midi encore on ......*
3. *Cet après-midi nous regardons un film, et demain après-midi aussi nous ...*
4. *Ce soir je retrouve mes copains, et demain soir également je ......*
5. *Puis on se couche vers dix heures, et la même chose demain, on ......*

Practice 20.2

Write these in French:

Example: he will leave ⇒ *il partira*

1. they will understand
2. we will (shall) choose
3. I will (shall) go out
4. you will get taller
5. she will drink
6. he will answer

Practice 20.3

Link the English and French:

Example: they will see = *ils verront*

1.	you will have to	(a)	*elle saura*
2.	he will have	(b)	*il aura*
3.	she will know (how to)	(c)	*vous ferez*
4.	I shall be able to	(d)	*nous viendrons*
5.	we shall come	(e)	*je pourrai*
6.	you will do	(f)	*tu devras*

Practice 20.4

Show which infinitives these future forms come from:

Example: *il sera (être / savoir)* ⇒ *être*

1. *nous irons (avoir / aller)*
2. *tu viendras (voir / venir)*
3. *j'aurai (avoir / être)*
4. *on verra (voir / aller)*
5. *vous ferez (finir / faire)*
6. *elle devra (devoir / donner)*
7. *ils sauront (être / savoir)*
8. *elles pourront (pouvoir / prendre)*

Practice 20.5

Choose the most suitable verb from the box below, to complete the dialogue:

Example: *Fred: Qu'est-ce que tu ...... cet été?* ⇒ *Qu'est-ce que tu **feras** cet été?*

Antoine:	J' ...... en Bretagne avec des copains.
Fred:	Vous ...... combien?
Antoine:	Il y ...... Michel, Pierre et moi, donc nous ...... trois. Malheureusement, Maryse ne ...... pas venir. Elle m'a dit qu'elle n' ...... pas d'argent et qu'elle ...... travailler pour son père.
Fred:	C'est vrai, ces vacances ...... chères, non?
Antoine:	Non, pas du tout, tu .... Nous ...... des économies, donc on ...... louer une voiture. Nous ...... nos sacs de couchage, alors nous ...... faire du camping.
Fred:	Tu ...... économiser beaucoup?
Antoine:	Oui, en effet. Mais dis donc!
Fred:	Quoi?
Antoine:	Est-ce que tu ...... libre au mois de juillet?
Fred:	Oh, je ne sais pas.
Antoine:	Quand est-ce que tu le ...... ? J'ai quelque chose à te proposer.
Fred:	Quoi?
Antoine:	Tu ...... en France avec nous?
Fred:	Non merci, je ...... me reposer chez moi!

~~feras~~	ferons	seras	serez	serons	seront	sauras
devra	devras	aura	aura	aurons	pourra	pourra
pourrons	viendras	voudrai	verras	irai		

Practice 20.6

Complete these sentences, using a suitable verb in the future tense. Give their English meaning:

Example: *Demain, j' ...... en France.* ⇒ *Demain, j'**irai** en France.* = Tomorrow, I will go to France.

1. *L'année prochaine, elle ...... dix-huit ans.*
2. *Ils ne ...... pas l'accompagner parce qu'ils n'ont pas d'argent.*
3. *Si tu travailles pendant dix heures, tu ...... fatigué.*
4. *Ce soir nous ...... le film au Rex.*
5. *Vous ...... au concert avec moi?*

Practice 20.7

Make this person making plans (saying 'I'm going to …') sound more determined (by changing it to 'I will …'). Say them aloud, pronouncing the strong gargling sound of the French '**r**':

Example: *Je vais partir à Paris* ⇒ *Je **partirai** à Paris.*

1. *Je vais voyager en Eurostar.*
2. *Ça va être rapide.*
3. *Je vais loger dans un hôtel au centre-ville.*
4. *Avec ma famille, nous allons visiter beaucoup de choses.*
5. *Nous allons manger des spécialités françaises.*
6. *Nous allons prendre le métro.*
7. *Nous allons voir la Tour Eiffel.*
8. *Nous allons pouvoir parler français.*
9. *Mes parents vont vouloir visiter des musées.*
10. *J'espère qu'il va faire beau.*

Chapter 21

Practice 21.1

Fill in the missing letters to complete these verbs in the perfect tense, then give the English meanings:

Example: *nous ...... regard -* ⇒ *nous **avons** regardé* = we (have) watched

1. *tu ...... aim......*
2. *on ...... mang......*
3. *j' ...... préfér......*
4. *vous ...... admi.......*
5. *ils ...... chant......*
6. *elle ...... écout......*

Practice 21.2

Change these –er verbs from the present to the perfect tense. As you write them, say them, remembering to smile to help you get your mouth in the right shape to pronounce the past participle properly:

Example: *Patrick joue au foot.* ⇒ *Patrick **a joué** au foot.*

1. *Angèle voyage en train.*
2. *Vous envoyez un mail.*
3. *Les Dawson habitent Paris.*
4. *Nous parlons français.*
5. *On apprécie le confort.*
6. *J'adore les croissants.*

Practice 21.3

Write these in French:

Example: they chose = *ils ont choisi*

1. she ran
2. we were able to
3. he had
4. you opened
5. I finished

Practice 21.4

Write these in French:

Example: he read ⇒ *il a lu*

1. I answered
2. they believed
3. you said
4. she was
5. we have waited
6. you wrote
7. he has taken
8. I put

Practice 21.5

Choose the correct alternative, then give the English meaning:

Example: *J'ai (pris / pu) regarder le nouveau James Bond.* = *J'ai **pu** regarder le nouveau James Bond.*
= I was able to watch the new James Bond.

1. *Il a (cru / couru) jusqu'à la gare.*
2. *Nous avons (dit / dû): 'Bon anniversaire!'*
3. *Ils ont (vu / voulu) aller en ville.*
4. *Elle a (plu / pris) son sac.*
5. *Tu as (eu / été) froid.*
6. *On a (fait / fini) du ski.*

Chapter 22

Practice 22.1

Choose the correct auxiliary, as appropriate, to complete the perfect tense of the verbs below. Give the English meaning:

Example: *Marie (a / est) allée en France.* ⇒ *Marie **est** allée en France.* = Marie went/has gone to France.

1. *Nous nous (avons / sommes) dépêchés pour prendre le train.*
2. *Mes amis (ont / sont) arrivés en retard.*
3. *Hier soir, elles (ont / sont) mangé au restaurant.*
4. *Tu (as / es) parti sans dire au revoir.*
5. *Vous (avez / êtes) voyagé en avion?*

Practice 22.2

Match the first and second parts of the sentences below, so that they make sense. Then give the English meaning:

Example: *Elle est sortie … dans son jardin.* = She went out into her garden.
Elle a sorti – ses clés. = She took out her keys.

1. *L'homme a monté*
2. *Mon frère est monté*
3. *Nous sommes rentrés*
4. *Tu as rentré*
5. *Elle s'est regardée*
6. *Elle a regardé*
7. *Je me suis levée*
8. *J'ai levé*

(a) *ses photos de vacances.*
(b) *tes affaires?*
(c) *l'escalier.*
(d) *jusqu' au premier étage.*
(e) *quand mon réveil a sonné.*
(f) *dans le miroir.*
(g) *mon petit frère.*
(h) *chez nous.*

Practice 22.3

Write out the story about Jeanine, adding agreements on the past participles where required. Take care: only the 'être' verbs will need an agreement!

Example: *Je m'appelle Jeanine. Je suis <u>allé</u> à la bibliothèque.* ⇒ *Je suis all**ée** à la bibliothèque.*

Quand je suis <u>entré</u> j'ai <u>remarqué</u> un jeune homme très beau. Il m'a <u>souri</u> et, je ne sais pas pourquoi, je me suis <u>approché</u> de lui.
'Je vous ai <u>vu</u> quelque part, n'est-ce pas?' ai-je <u>dit</u>.
Il a <u>hésité</u> un instant, puis il a <u>répondu</u>:
'Oui, nous nous sommes <u>rencontré</u> la semaine dernière chez Nicolas. J'y suis <u>allé</u> avec ma petite amie Ludivine, mais nous nous sommes <u>disputé</u> quand elle a <u>vu</u> que je vous regardais. J'ai <u>voulu</u> vous parler, mais elle s'est <u>fâché</u> et elle m'a <u>abandonné</u>.'

Practice 22.4

Now complete the rest of Jeanine's story by giving the correct form of the perfect tense of the verbs in brackets. If a verb is not one of the small group taking *être*, assume it takes *avoir*. If it takes *être*, remember the past participle agreement:

Example: *Je (rire).* ⇒ *J'**ai ri**.*

Je lui (dire): 'Pourquoi est-ce que vous ne m' pas (demander) de danser quand votre copine (partir)?'
Il (rougir), puis il (se décider): 'Est-ce que vous (faire) du saut à l'élastique? C'est passionnant.'
Nous (se regarder), l'amour dans les yeux. Et voilà comment notre histoire (commencer)!

Chapter 23

Practice 23.1

If you had to turn these sentences into French (don't worry, you don't have to!), would you use the perfect (perf.) or the imperfect (imp.), and why?

Example: Last night she <u>sang</u> beautifully. ⇒ perf: (applies to one occasion, story line.)
She always <u>sang</u> beautifully. ⇒ imp: (regularly in the past, background information.)

1. I <u>watched</u> TV for three hours.
2. While I <u>watched</u> TV, the phone <u>rang</u>.
3. She <u>was</u> ten when her family <u>moved</u> house.
4. When they <u>were moving</u> house, they <u>lost</u> their cat.
5. My brother <u>spent</u> ten years in Paris.
6. While he <u>was</u> there, he <u>worked</u> for Renault.
7. Life <u>used to be</u> simple when I <u>was</u> young.
8. Things <u>became</u> more difficult when I <u>got married</u>.

Practice 23.2

Match each pronoun below with its correct imperfect verb form, then give the English meanings:

Example: *je –* ⇒ *je finissais* = I was finishing / I used to finish / I finished

1. *tu*   (a) *choisissiez*
2. *il*   (b) *vendaient*
3. *nous*   (c) *prenions*
4. *vous*   (d) *buvait*
5. *ils*   (e) *donnais*

Practice 23.3

Some of the verbs below are in the present, some in the future, some in the perfect. Change them into the imperfect. It will help you if you think of their infinitive first:

Example: *Nous partirons au Portugal. (partir)* ⇒ *Nous **partions** au Portugal.*

1. *Elles sont contentes.*
2. *Ils finissent leur match.*
3. *Tu vas à la fête?*
4. *Tout le monde préfère les vacances au travail.*
5. *Je ne fais pas de ski.*
6. *Ma voisine voudra nous inviter.*
7. *Vous irez au centre-ville.*
8. *Je prendrai le métro.*
9. *Les chanteurs donneront un concert tous les soirs.*
10. *Pourquoi est-ce que tu seras à Lyon cet été?*
11. *Vous n'avez pas répondu.*
12. *Daniel s'est préparé à toute vitesse.*
13. *On est monté à la Tour Eiffel.*
14. *Nous avons bu du Champagne.*
15. *J'ai dû rentrer chez moi.*

Practice 23.4

Complete the following story by choosing the most suitable verb from the box:

Example: *Quand j' ...... quatorze ans, je ...... en France en voyage scolaire. = Quand j'**avais** quatorze ans, je **suis allé** en France en voyage scolaire.*

J' ...... dix jours chez mon correspondant, qui ...... en Bretagne. La nourriture ...... excellente, et j' ...... du vin pour la première fois. Il ...... très fort!
Chaque jour, nous ...... une excursion dans la région. Madame Beraud ...... plus vite que ma mère. Elle m' ...... beaucoup d'endroits intéressants. Un jour, nous ...... au Mont Saint Michel. Il y ...... beaucoup de touristes.
Après dix jours, j' ...... rentrer en Angleterre, et j' ...... un peu triste. Pendant mon séjour, j' ...... beaucoup de photos et, le jour de mon départ, la famille m' ...... du vin. Les bouteilles ...... lourdes! Heureusement j' ...... la douane sans problème, mais quand je ...... chez moi, j' ...... qu'une des bouteilles ...... cassée, et que tous mes vêtements ...... tachés.

~~avais~~	avait	habitait	était	était	était
étais	étaient	étaient	conduisait	ai dû	sommes allés
avons fait	ai pris	ai passé	ai passé	ai découvert	suis arrivé
~~suis allé~~	ai bu	a montré	a offert		

Practice 23.5

An imperfect ending? In the following story, choose the correct tense of the verb. The agreements of the past participles of *être* verbs have also been missed out. Put them back where appropriate:

Example: *Nous (lisions / avons lu) cette histoire dans le journal, et nous nous (sentions / sommes senti) tristes parce que nous (connaissions / avons connu) madame Marquet. ⇒ Nous **avons lu** cette histoire dans le journal, et nous nous **sommes sentis** tristes parce que nous **connaissions** madame Marquet.*

Il (était / a été) neuf heures du soir et il (faisait / a fait) nuit. Madame Marquet, une vieille dame plutôt sourde qui (vivait / a vécu) seule, (décidait / a décidé) d'acheter des provisions au petit magasin qui (se trouvait / s'est trouvé) en face de chez elle. Elle (sortait / est sorti) très vite de son appartement parce que le magasin (était / a été) sur le point de fermer. A cette heure, il (n'y avait pas / n'y a pas eu) beaucoup de circulation d'habitude, donc elle (ne regardait pas / n'a pas regardé) pour voir s'il y (avait / a eu) des voitures qui (s'approchaient / se sont approché). Elle (commençait / a commencé) à traverser la rue. Elle (n'entendait pas / n'a pas entendu) le moteur d'un gros camion qui (roulait / a roulé) assez vite vers elle ...

Practice 23.6

Now, to complete the above story, choose for each gap the most suitable infinitive from the box. Put it in the imperfect or perfect, as appropriate. Remember to add agreements where appropriate:

Example: *Nous ...... à lire. L'article ...... de cette façon: = Nous **avons continué** à lire. L'article **finissait** de cette façon:*

Madame Marquet ...... au milieu de la rue quand le camion .... A la dernière seconde, le camionneur, qui ...... fatigué, ... Madame Marquet. Il ...... de freiner, mais c' ...... trop tard! Le camion ...... en collision avec la pauvre dame, qui ...... et ...... immobile. Le camionneur, qui ...... peur de perdre son emploi si on ...... qu'il ...... responsable de l'accident, ... sans s'arrêter. On ...... madame Marquet le lendemain matin – morte.

être	être	être	être	trouver	partir
voir	avoir	~~finir~~	entrer	tomber	~~continuer~~
essayer	arriver	rester	penser		

Chapter 24

Practice 24.1

Change these *'est-ce que'* questions into 'intonation only' questions. Say them aloud, making sure you raise your voice at the end:

Example: *Est-ce que ta sœur est rentrée?* ⇒ *Ta sœur est rentrée?*

1. *Est-ce qu'elle a passé de bonnes vacances?*
2. *Est-ce que tu partiras avec elle l'année prochaine?*
3. *Est-ce que tes parents seront d'accord?*
4. *Est-ce que vous resterez au même endroit?*
5. *Est-ce que je pourrai venir aussi?*

Practice 24.2

Change these 'intonation only' questions into easier *'est-ce que'* questions. Say them aloud, making sure you raise your voice at the end:

Example: *Tu as vu le film où?* ⇒ *Où est-ce que tu as vu le film?*

1. *Tu y es allé avec qui?*
2. *Vous avez payé combien?*
3. *C'était quoi comme film?*
4. *Tu préfères les films d'horreur, pourquoi?*
5. *Vous êtes allés au cinéma quand?*

Practice 24.3

Change these inversion questions into easier *'est-ce que'* questions. Say them aloud, making sure you raise your voice at the end:

Example: *Pourquoi regardes-tu toujours le foot à la télé?* ⇒ *Pourquoi est-ce que tu regardes toujours le foot à la télé?*

1. *Quelle équipe supportes-tu?*
2. *Comment s'entraînent-ils?*
3. *Quand sera le prochain match?*
4. *Où vont-ils jouer?*
5. *Qui va gagner?*

Practice 24.4

Change these questions into inversion questions, if possible. Take care: some cannot be inverted, some will need an extra *'t'*, and some will need an extra pronoun:

Examples: *Est-ce que je veux vraiment sortir avec Marianne?* ⇒ *Est-ce que je veux vraiment sortir avec Marianne?*
On va aller où? ⇒ *Où va-t-on aller?*

1. *Ou bien, est-ce que je préfère sortir avec Angélique?*
2. *Et est-ce qu'Angélique voudra sortir avec moi?*
3. *Est-ce que je suis assez charmant pour elle?*
4. *On va faire quoi?*
5. *Est-ce que j'ai assez d'argent pour l'emmener manger chez Maxim?*

Practice 24.5

Unjumble these questions:

Example: *voiture - t - acheter il Quelle va?* ⇒ *Quelle voiture va-t-il acheter?*

1. *places Combien de ils réserver - vont?*
2. *Pourquoi Cédric elle aime pas - t - n' Mylène?*
3. *elle sort qui ce - Avec soir?*
4. *Que les vacances faire - t - il pendant grandes va?*
5. *je peux française est la grammaire - apprendre que ce Comment?*

Chapter 25

Practice 25.1

These sentences don't make sense as they are. Make them negative so that they do:

Example: *Un ballon de rugby est rond* = *Un ballon de rugby **n'est pas** rond.*

1. *Les footballeurs sont toujours très intelligents.*
2. *Nous sommes allés faire du ski à Paris.*
3. *J'irai en vacances sur la lune l'année prochaine.*
4. *L'année dernière, ils ont traversé le désert en bateau.*
5. *Il fait plus chaud en Suède qu'au Mexique.*

Practice 25.2

Match the questions and answers:

Example: *Tu as une vie sociale très active?* ⇒ *Non, je ne sors jamais.*

1. *Où es-tu sortie le week-end dernier?*
2. *Comment as-tu passé le temps?*
3. *Avec qui as-tu discuté?*
4. *Qui est-ce que tu as rencontré?*
5. *Tu es contente de ta vie?*
6. *Tu as encore des copains?*

   (a) *Non, elle n'est pas idéale.*
   (b) *Je n'ai rien fait.*
   (c) *Je ne suis allée nulle part.*
   (d) *Non, je n'ai plus d'amis.*
   (e) *Je n'ai vu que mes parents.*
   (f) *Je n'ai parlé à personne.*

Practice 25.3

Aisha is trying to chat up Frédéric but is not having much success, as Frédéric just mumbles one-word answers. Give his short negative answers to the following questions:

Example: *Tu vas souvent au cinéma?* ⇒ *Non.*

1. *Avec qui sors-tu en ce moment?*
2. *Qu'est-ce que tu fais ce soir?*
3. *Combien de fois es-tu allé au nouveau club?*
4. *Qui t'a invité à danser?*
5. *Qu'est-ce que je peux faire pour te persuader à sortir avec moi?*

Practice 25.4

Tintin is reading an advert about Belgium (his country), but he does not agree with it at all. Write his version, making every statement negative, as suggested by the English words in brackets. Remember that in a negative sentence, *du, de la, de l'* and *des* become *de* or *d'*:

Example: *La Belgique est un des pays les plus intéressants du monde!* (not)
⇒ *La Belgique **n'est pas** un des pays les plus intéressants du monde!*

1. *Tous les chemins mènent à Bruxelles!* (not)
2. *On trouve toujours quelque chose à faire.* (never anything)
3. *Tout le monde est sympathique.* (nobody)
4. *La cuisine est toujours délicieuse.* (never)
5. *On trouve des restaurants partout.* (nowhere)
6. *Ils servent des moules-frites.* (only)
7. *Il y a des musées intéressants et aussi des monuments historiques.* (neither ... nor)
8. *Quand on a visité la Belgique, on veut encore y retourner.* (no more / not again)

Chapter 26

Practice 26.1

Show whether the underlined words are subjects (subj.), direct objects (dir. obj.), or indirect objects (ind. obj.):

        (Subj.)   (Dir.obj.)

Example: *Serge* fait *des projets* pour ses vacances.

1. *Il* regarde *les destinations* sur internet.
2. *Il* parle *à son frère* avant de se décider.
3. Puis *il* demande *à son copain* Henri s'*il* veut *l'*accompagner.
4. *Henri* est d'accord. *Ils* iront en Normandie.
5. *Ils* réservent *leurs places* et commencent à préparer *leurs valises*.

Practice 26.2

Fill in the missing subject, direct object and indirect object pronouns, from the list below:

Example: *La télé? .... regardons tous les soirs.* ⇒ *La télé?* **Nous la** *regardons tous les soirs.*
1. *Edith choisit un CD, puis .... achète.*
2. *Les enfants disent 'Bon anniversaire' à leur mère, puis .... donnent des fleurs.*
3. *...... voulez ce magazine? ...... pouvez ...... prendre, ... ai fini de ...... lire.*
4. *Où as- ...... trouvé ce joli pull? ...... vais te ...... emprunter, si ...... veux bien!*
5. *Isabelle n'a pas dit à ses parents où ...... sortait. Elle ne ...... a pas dit la vérité.*

tu	tu	leur	l'	j'	l'	vous	vous	~~nous~~
lui	ils	je	elle	elle	le	le	~~la~~	

Practice 26.3

Unjumble the following sentences, taking care with the position of pronouns:

Example: *ai lui Je un donné cadeau.* ⇒ *Je lui ai donné un cadeau.*
1. *ne regardé Elle a pas l'.*
2. *nous ont téléphoné m' amis Mes discuté et avons.*
3. *Pour une carte lui anniversaire ils son écriront.*
4. *Il apporte quelque Cédric toujours m' ici vient chose quand.*
5. *tu venir à piscine nous la Préfères- avec?*

Practice 26.4

Rewrite the following sentences, replacing the words underlined by the appropriate pronouns (make sure you put them in the right place!):

Example: *Marie regarde la télé tous les soirs.* ⇒ **Elle la** *regarde tous les soirs.*

1. *Ses émissions favorites sont les comédies, qui plaisent beaucoup à Marie.*
2. *Son père dit à Marie de lire ou de jouer avec son frère.*
3. *Marie et son frère n'écoutent pas leur père.*
4. *Quand leur copain Boris vient, ils téléphonent à leurs cousins. Ils demandent à leurs cousins de venir.*
5. *Leurs cousins viennent chercher Marie, son frère et leurs copains.*

Practice 26.5

Translate these English sentences into French:

Examples:
Mrs Hubbard gave her dog a bone. = *Mme. Hubbard a donné un os à son chien.*
Mrs Hubbard gave her dog to her son. ⇒ *Mme. Hubbard a donné son chien à son fils.*

1. She sent him a letter.
2. She sent him to the shops.
3. She always cooks them a meal.
4. She always cooks them very well.
5. We bought him a new CD.
6. We bought him at the pet shop. (the pet shop – *l'animalerie*)
7. They will bring it a new toy. (to bring – *apporter*)
8. They will bring it to our house.
9. I'm going to lend them this book. (to lend – *prêter*)
10. I'm going to lend them to my girlfriend.

Practice 26.6

Complete the following with an emphatic pronoun:

Example: *......, ils sont riches!* (them) ⇒ ***Eux, ils sont riches!***

1. *C'est confortable chez ......!* (us)
2. *Viens à côté de ......!* (me)
3. *Il est beau, ...!* (him)
4. *Elle est super, ...!* (her)
5. *Et ......, comment t'appelles-tu?* (you)

Practice 26.7

Find the most suitable answer for each of these questions, filling in *y* or *en* as appropriate. Then give the English meaning:

Example: *Tu as des copains? - Oui, j' ...... ai beaucoup.* ⇒ *Oui, j'**en** ai beaucoup.* = Yes, I have a lot.
Tu vas en France souvent? - Oui, j'......vais souvent. ⇒ *Oui, j'**y** vais souvent.* = Yes, I go there often.

1.	*Combien d'argent as-tu apporté?*	(a)	*Oui, il ... loue un appartement.*
2.	*Est-ce qu'il fait de la planche à voile?*	(b)	*J' ... ai apporté beaucoup.*
3.	*Est-ce qu'il aime les chats?*	(c)	*Seulement quand il ... a du vent.*
4.	*Habite-t-il à Paris?*	(d)	*Oui, il ... ... a trop!*
5.	*Il y a des tas d'exercices dans ce livre?*	(e)	*Non, il ... a peur!*

Practice 26.8

Read what your new French friend, whom you met on holiday, is saying or asking, then give her a reply, following the suggestions in brackets and using pronouns to avoid repetitions:

Example: *Moi, j'ai quinze ans, et toi?* – (I am sixteen) ⇒ *Moi, j'en ai seize.*

1. *Je suis arrivée à Biarritz mardi dernier, et toi?* – (I arrived there two days ago.)
2. *Moi, j'ai un frère.* – (I have two (of them).)
3. *J'adore aller à la plage, et toi?* – (I like going there too.)
4. *Voudrais-tu rencontrer mes copains?* – (Yes, I would really like to meet them.)
5. *Est-ce que tu veux demander à tes frères de venir aussi?* – (Yes, I am going to ask them.)
6. *On pourrait aller voir le dernier 'James Bond'.* – (Yes, we have not seen it yet.)
7. *Où vas-tu passer tes vacances l'été prochain?* – (I hope to spend them here.)
8. *Je vais revenir ici aussi.* – (Great! We will see each other, I hope.)
9. *Tu m'enverras des mails, n'est-ce pas?* – (Yes, and you will write to me, too!)
10. *Si tu veux, tu peux venir me voir.* – (Thank you, and you can come to my place, too.)

Practice 26.9

Improve these sentences by removing the repetitions, first using subject and direct object pronouns, then using relative pronouns:

Example: *Ecoute ce CD. J'adore ce CD.* ⇒ *Ecoute ce CD. Je l'adore.* ⇒ *Ecoute ce CD **que** j'adore.*

1. *Je te présente madame Chirac. Madame Chirac est ma voisine.*
2. *Il mange le poulet. Elle a préparé le poulet.*
3. *Nicole se décide pour les vacances en camping. Les vacances en camping sont moins chères.*
4. *Tu ne vas pas au cinéma Panécran? Le cinéma Panécran est tout près.*
5. *Où est le journal? Tu as acheté le journal ce matin.*

Practice 26.10

Fill the gaps with *qui, que* or *qu'*, as appropriate:

Example: *Je vais te montrer le jean … j'ai acheté aujourd'hui.* ⇒ *Je vais te montrer le jean **que** j'ai acheté aujourd'hui.*

C'est un nouveau modèle … est très confortable. Il a des boutons … sont en métal, et des poches … je trouve bien pratiques. Le premier jean … je voulais était trop grand, mais le vendeur, … je connais et … est très aimable, m'en a apporté un autre … était plus petit. Ma sœur a acheté le même pour aller avec le pull … elle a acheté récemment.

Practice 26.11

Now give the English version of the story in Exercise 26.10 above. What do you notice about the English equivalents of *qui* and *que/qu'*?

Example: *Je vais te montrer le jean que j'ai acheté aujourd'hui.* ⇒ I'm going to show you the jeans (that) I bought today.

Practice 26.12

We would like to know what you think of 'Skeleton French'. Please answer this questionnaire. We had no time to proofread this last page, but we believe there is one mistake in each question and each answer (!) Can you spot them?

Example: *A ton avis, ce livre est-t-il utile?*   ⇒   est-il
(a) *Oui, très utiles.*   ⇒   très utile
(b) *Non, pas très. Je savait déjà tout ça.*   ⇒   je savais
(c) *Non, pas du tout. Je n'est rien compris.*   ⇒   je n'ai rien

1. *Est-ce que les explications étaient clair?*
   (a) *Oui, tout étaient très clair.*
   (b) *En general, pas mal.*
   (c) *Non, absolument pas. S'était confus.*

2. *As-tu trouver les exercices faciles?*
   (a) *Oui, assez facile.*
   (b) *Oui, beaucoup trop faciles pour me.*
   (c) *Non, je n'ai pas pus les faire.*

3. *Est-ce qu'il en avait assez d'exercices?*
   (a) *Oui, le nombres juste.*
   (b) *Non, trop. C'était vraiment ennuyeuses.*
   (c) *Non, je veut deux fois plus d'exercices.*

4. *Qu'est-ce que tu as pense des dessins?*
   (a) *Elles étaient amusants.*
   (b) *Ils étaient plutôt stupides, pour les enfants jeunes.*
   (c) *Je ne ai pas vraiment remarqué les dessins.*

5. *Est-ce que tu recommandera ce livre?*
   (a) *Oui, certainement, à mon copains.*
   (b) *Non, sait une perte de temps.*
   (c) *Non, la grammaire francaise est trop difficile.*

Skeleton Key: Answers to the exercises

Practice 1.1

1. N = cinema. 2. V = to watch. 3. N = ticket. 4. N = squares/seats.
5. V = to return/go back. 6. N - film.

Practice 1.2

1. *le – article* = I'm eating the cake. 2. *bonbons – noun* = She likes the sweets. 3. *préférez – verb* = Do you prefer the fish or the chicken? 4. *grande – adjective* = Here is a big box of chocolates for you. 5. *et – conjunction* = He orders a pizza and a coke. 6. *au – preposition* = We are going to the restaurant.
7. *tu – pronoun* = And (what about) you? Do you like coffee? 8. *silencieusement – adverb* = They read silently.

Practice 1.3

1. noun, verb, noun 2. pronoun, verb, article, adjective, noun 3. pronoun, verb, adjective, preposition, preposition, article, noun 4. noun, verb, verb, preposition, article, noun 5. pronoun, verb, preposition, adjective, noun

Practice 1.4

1. *La Tour Eiffel est formidable.* 2. *Il fait beau dans le sud.* 3. *Paris est la capitale de la France.*
4. *J'aime la musique italienne.* 5. *Je pars en vacances avec mes copains.*

Practice 2.1

1. M 2. ? 3. F 4. M 5. F 6. ? 7. ? 8. M 9. M 10. M

Practice 2.2

1. *un avion = a plane; deux avions = two planes* 2. *une voiture = a car; deux voitures = two cars*
3. *un hélicoptère = a helicopter; deux hélicoptères = two helicopters* 4. *un vélo = a bicycle; deux vélos = two bicycles* 5. *une mobylette = a moped; deux mobylettes = two mopeds*

Practice 2.3

1. *les manteaux = the coats* 2. *des fez = some fezes* 3. *des tas = lots/heaps* 4. *les chevaux = the horses* 5. *les cheveux = the hair(s)*

Practice 3.1

1. an artist 2. a (female) secretary 3. (some) assistants 4. *un village* 5. *une maison* 6. *des villes*

Practice 3.2

1. the foot 2. the hand 3. the ear 4. the eyes 5. *le chemisier* 6. *la chemise* 7. *l'anorak*
8. *les chaussures*

Practice 4.1

1. *une salade verte* 2. *une banane jaune* 3. *une mauvaise pomme* 4. *une pêche mûre*

Practice 4.2

1. *des cochons roses* 2. *des vaches brunes* 3. *les chiens méchants* 4. *les souris timides*
5. *des animaux domestiques*

Practice 4.3

1. *ma sœur* 2. *mon cousin Pierre* 3. *mes amis* 4. *mes sœurs* 5. *mon ami Henri* 6. *ma robe*

Practice 4.4

1. *ton oncle* 2. *tes parents* 3. *ta télévision* 4. *ton costume* 5. *ta cousine Angélique* 6. *tes frères*

Practice 4.5

1. *sa voiture* 2. *sa voiture* 3. *son ami* 4. *ses amis* 5. *ses os* 6. *ses os*

Practice 4.6

Je suis dans mon lit. Mon chien Bruno entre dans ma chambre. Il veut son petit déjeuner. Je mets mes lunettes et je regarde mon réveil: 5 heures!
'Bruno! Retourne dans ton lit! Ton petit déjeuner est à 7 heures 30, et après, c'est ta promenade. Tes amis sont là, dans le parc, surtout ta petite amie Brunette. Tu es content?'
Et Bruno agite sa queue!
I am in (my) bed. My dog Bruno comes into my (bed)room. He wants his breakfast. I put on my glasses and look at my alarm clock: 5 o'clock!
'Bruno! Go back to (your) bed! Your breakfast is at 7.30, and then, it's (time for) your walk. Your friends are there, in the park, especially your girlfriend Brunette. Are you pleased?'
And Bruno wags his tail!

Practice 5.1

1. *j'aime, il aime, elle aime, on aime* 2. *tu parles* 3. *je regarde, il regarde, elle regarde, on regarde*
4. *vous écoutez* 5. *ils cherchent, elles cherchent* 6. *nous jouons*

Practice 5.2

1. *je joue* = I play/I am playing 2. *nous regardons* = we watch/we are watching 3. *elles écoutent* = they listen/they are listening 4. *tu cherches* = you look for/you are looking for 5. *vous aimez* = you like
6. *ils parlent* = they speak/they are speaking

Practice 5.3

1. *on est* = one is (we/you/they are) 2. *vous êtes* = you are 3. *tu es* = you are 4. *elle est* = she is 5. *nous sommes* = we are 6. *ils sont* = they are

Practice 5.4

1. *tu as* = you have 2. *les amis ont* = the friends have 3. *on a* = one has (we/you/they have) 4. *nous avons* = we have 5. *vous avez* = you have 6. *j'ai* = I have 7. *Frank a froid* = Frank is cold 8. *mes parents ont raison* = my parents are right 9. *j'ai faim* = I am hungry 10. *mon frère a vingt ans* = my brother is twenty

Practice 5.5

1. *Loïc va* = Loïc goes 2. *vous allez* = you go 3. *je vais* = I go 4. *mes cousines vont* = my cousins go
5. *tu vas* = you go 6. *on va* = one goes (we/you/they go)

Practice 5.6

1. *on fait* = one does/makes (we/you/they do/make) 2. *mon copain et moi (nous) faisons* = My friend and I (we) do/make 3. *je fais* = I do/make 4. *vous faites* = you do/make 5. *son chien fait* = his/her dog does/makes 6. *ses chats font* = his/her cats do/make

Practice 5.7

1. *on prend* = one takes (we/you/they take) 2. *tu prends* = you take 3. *je prends* = I take 4. *nous prenons* = we take 5. *Esther et Céline prennent* = Esther and Céline take 6. *ton oncle prend* = your uncle takes

Practice 5.8

1. *Le bébé a trois dents* = The baby has three teeth. 2. *Nous allons au cinéma en voiture* = We are going to the cinema in the car. 3. *Je suis fatigué* = I am tired. 4. *Marie a seize ans* = Marie is sixteen. 5. *Il fait chaud, donc il a chaud* = It is hot, so he is hot. 6. *Tu prends le train ou l'avion?* = Are you taking the train or the plane? 7. *Elles vont en autobus* = They go by bus. 8. *On prend un café?* = Shall we have (take) a coffee? 9. *Vous êtes américain?* = Are you American? 10. *Les garçons font de la natation* = The boys swim (literally: do swimming).

Practice 5.9
1. *Jouons au tennis!* 2. *Ecoute le CD!* 3. *Restez ici!* 4. *Regarde les photos!* 5. *Allons à Paris!* 6. *Faites une omelette!*

Practice 6.1
1. *Demain, Marie va partir en voyage* = Tomorrow, Marie is going to go on a trip. 2. *Nous allons acheter des CD* = We are going to buy some CDs. 3. *Tu vas faire du ski* = You are going to ski. 4. *Vous allez écrire un mail* = You are going to write an e-mail. 5. *On va regarder un DVD* = We are going to watch a DVD. 6. *Eric va jouer au football* = Eric is going to play football. 7. *Michel et Caroline vont aller au restaurant* = Michel and Caroline are going to go to the restaurant.

Practice 6.2
1. *Demain, il va faire du ski nautique.* 2. *Demain, elle va préparer des crêpes.* 3. *Demain, ils vont jouer au golf.* 4. *Demain, nous allons aller au match.* 5. *Demain, on va finir le livre.*

Practice 7.1
1. *décider, je décide, elle a décidé* 2. *cinéma* 3. *répétition* 4. *Céline* 5. *tu as écouté, il écoute, vous écoutez*

Practice 7.2
1. *elle achète* 2. *Hélène* 3. *tu répètes* 4. *frère* 5. *règle* 6. *vous appelez* 7. *nous achetons* 8. *on jette*

Practice 7.3
1. *fête* 2. *arrêter* 3. *honnête* 4. *quête* 5. *pâtes*

Practice 7.4
1. *plâtre* 2. *coûter* 3. *mât* 4. *août* 5. *maître*

Practice 7.5
1. *hâte* = haste 2. *pâté* = paste 3. *tâche* = task 4. *rôti* = roast 5. *croûte* = crust

Practice 8.1
1. *Nous avons regardé la télé* = We watched TV. 2. *Il a parlé avec ses amis* = He spoke with his friends. 3. *Les filles ont adoré le concert* = The girls loved the concert. 4. *Tu as aimé le film?* = Did you like the film? 5. *Vous avez déjà mangé?* = Have you eaten yet (already)?

Practice 8.2
1. *Je préfère la limonade au lait.* Pres. 2. *Michel a donné un cadeau à son amie.* Perf. 3. *Nous avons nagé dans la mer.* Perf. 4. *Vous avez trouvé vos lunettes?* Perf. 5. *Où est-ce que tu habites?* Pres. 6. *Tu restes dans un hôtel?* Pres. 7. *Je pense, donc je suis … fatigué.* Pres. 8. *Elle a oublié son billet.* Perf. 9. *Ils ont refusé de partir.* Perf. 10. *Il a répété la question trois fois.* Perf.

Practice 8.3
1. *Marie-Ange a pris un sac à dos.* 2. *Nadine et Aïsha ont fait les courses.* 3. *Vous avez fait du vélo.* 4. *J'ai pris le train.* 5. *Sylvie et moi (nous) avons fait de l'équitation.* 6. *On a pris un café.* 7. *Elle a pris son temps.* 8. *Tu as fait la cuisine.*

Practice 8.4
1. *Jean est allé en ville.* 2. *Nous sommes allés au gymnase.* 3. *Alain et toi, vous êtes allés en Belgique?* 4. *On est allé au parc.* 5. *Tu es allé(e) à la piscine.* 6. *Je suis allé(e) à Genève.*

Practice 8.5
1. *Il avait les cheveux roux.* 2. *Il était vachement beau.* 3. *Il avait environ 30 ans.* 4. *Moi, j'étais complètement excité(e).* 5. *J'avais des difficultés à parler.* 6. *Il avait un pantalon très chic.* 7. *Ses chaussures avaient des lacets roses.* 8. *Il était vraiment sympa.* 9. *Ses chansons étaient super cool.* 10. *Il y avait énormément de fans au concert.*

Practice 8.6

Je suis allé(e) à la plage. J'ai retrouvé mes copains. Nous avons joué au volley. Puis nous avons décidé de nager dans la mer. L'eau était froide. J'ai passé une bonne journée et j'étais bien content(e).
I went to the beach. I met (up with) my friends. We played volleyball. Then we decided to swim in the sea. The water was cold. I had a good day and I was very happy.

Practice 8.7

1. *Les joueurs de foot arrivent au stade.* Pres. 2. *Vous allez acheter des glaces.* Fut. 3. *Tu aimes le poulet?* Pres. 4. *Elle a changé de place.* Perf. 5. *Nous sommes allés en Suisse.* Perf. 6. *Patrick va partir à 8 heures.* Fut. 7. *Il a une nouvelle moto.* Pres. 8. *Ils sont très grands.* Pres. 9. *Vous avez acheté beaucoup de choses?* Perf. 10. *Je vais au match de tennis.* Pres.

Practice 8.8

1. *actuellement* = (h) at the moment. 2. *aujourd'hui* = (i) today. 3. *demain* = (c) tomorrow. 4. *dans dix jours* = (b) in ten days' time. 5. *maintenant* = (g) now. 6. *il y a trois jours* = (j) three days ago. 7. *hier* = (a) yesterday. 8. *l'année prochaine* = (f) next year. 9. *après-demain* = (d) the day after tomorrow. 10. *la semaine dernière* = (e) last week.

1. *Aujourd'hui je mange à la maison, mais hier j'ai mangé au restaurant.* 2. *La semaine dernière, il est allé à Londres, mais après-demain il va aller à Glasgow.* 3. *L'année prochaine, nous allons visiter le Maroc, mais maintenant nous visitons la Tunisie.* 4. *Il y a trois jours, elles ont acheté des vêtements, mais demain, elles vont acheter des chaussures.*

Practice 9.1

1. *Est-ce qu'elle est allée à la gare?* 2. *Est-ce que vous avez déjà visité Bruxelles?* 3. *Est-ce qu'ils vont acheter une grande voiture?* 4. *Est-ce qu'Emmanuelle va partir bientôt?* 5. *Est-ce que les Français mangent des escargots?*

Practice 9.2

1. *Avec qui est-ce que tu es allé?* = Who did you go with?/With whom did you go? 2. *Pourquoi est-ce que tu aimes la France?* = Why do you like France? 3. *Quand est-ce que tu vas en vacances? La semaine prochaine?* = When are you going on holiday? Next week? 4. *Combien de temps est-ce que le film a duré?* = How long did the film last? 5. *Comment est-ce que tu as fait le trajet? En avion?* = How did you travel/make the journey? By plane? 6. *Qu'est-ce que tu as fait hier soir?* = What did you do last night? 7. *Combien est-ce que tu as payé cette robe? Plus de 100 €?* = How much did you pay for this dress? More than 100 €? 8. *Quel chemisier est-ce que tu préfères?* = Which blouse do you prefer? 9. *A quelle heure est-ce que tu es allé au match?* = (At) what time did you go to the match? 10. *Est-ce que tu sais où il est allé?* = Do you know where he went?

Practice 10.1

1. *Pierre n'est pas petit.* 2. *Elles n'écoutent pas la musique.* 3. *Nous ne regardons pas les DVD.* 4. *Tu ne vas pas au cinéma?* 5. *Vous n'aimez pas le fromage?*

Practice 10.2

1. *On n'est pas allé à la pâtisserie.* 2. *Les Anglais n'ont pas aimé les cuisses de grenouille.* 3. *Elles n'ont pas acheté la plus belle boîte de chocolats.* 4. *Edith n'a pas chanté sa dernière chanson.* 5. *Il n'a pas fait froid.*

Practice 11.1

C'était ma première visite au Canada. D'habitude, je passe mes vacances en France, à Bordeaux, ou en Espagne, et une fois je suis allé aux Etats-Unis. A l'aéroport, j'ai montré mon passeport au douanier. Je suis très vite arrivé à mon hôtel en taxi, parce que le chauffeur ne s'est pas arrêté aux feux!
It was my first visit to Canada. Usually, I spend my holidays in France, in Bordeaux, or in Spain, and once (one time) I went to the USA. At the airport, I showed my passport to the Customs' officer. I very quickly arrived at my hotel by taxi, because the driver did not stop at the lights!

Practice 11.2

Plus tard je suis sorti de l'hôtel pour visiter les attractions de la ville. J'ai consulté l'horaire des autobus. Il y en avait un qui partait du coin de la rue. J'ai vu beaucoup de gens qui rentraient du bureau, ou qui regardaient les vitrines des magasins du centre. Près de la gare, il y avait un petit parc d'attractions. Later I went out of the hotel to visit the city sights. I checked the bus timetable. There was one leaving from the corner of the street. I saw a lot of people who were returning home from the office, or who were looking at the shop windows in the centre. Near the station there was a small amusement park.

Practice 11.3

1. *le jardin de la dame* 2. *la maison du docteur* 3. *l'anniversaire de ma sœur* 4. *les livres de l'étudiant*
5. *les livres des étudiants*

Practice 11.4

Est-ce que vous avez des tomates? Est-ce que vous avez de la purée de tomates? Est-ce que vous avez du fromage? Est-ce que vous avez des olives? Est-ce que vous avez des anchois? Est-ce que vous avez de l'huile? Est-ce que vous avez du sel et du poivre?

Practice 11.5

1. *Vous n'avez pas de purée de tomates.* 2. *Vous n'avez pas de fromage.* 3. *Vous n'avez pas d'anchois.*

Practice 11.6

1. *Paris est en France* = Paris is in France. 2. *Nous allons prendre le tunnel sous la Manche* = We are going to take the Channel tunnel (literally: under the Channel). 3. *Mon frère est parti sans moi* = My brother left without me. 4. *Elle est rentrée avant dix heures* = She returned before ten.
5. *Mes amis ont acheté un appartement à Glasgow* = My friends bought a flat in Glasgow. 6. *Marie va en vacances avec ses parents* = Marie goes on holiday with her parents. 7. *Le cinéma est entre le restaurant et le complexe multisports* = The cinema is between the restaurant and the sports centre.
8. *Avant le déjeuner, il a téléphoné à son copain* = Before lunch, he telephoned his friend.

Practice 11.7

1. *La semaine prochaine, nous allons partir en France pour trois jours* = Next week, we will go to France for three days. 2. *Mes cousins sont restés chez moi pendant une semaine* = My cousins stayed at my place for a week. 3. *Elle habite ici depuis cinq ans* = She has been living here for five years. 4. *J'ai habité à Paris pendant deux ans* = I lived in Paris for two years. 5. *Le footballeur ne va pas jouer pour huit mois* = The footballer is not going to play for eight months.

Practice 12.1

1. *Il s'appelle Minou* = It is called Minou. 2. *Il aime les oiseaux* = It likes (the) birds. 3. *Ils habitent dans une cage* = They live in a cage. 4. *Elle est blanche et bleue* = It is white and blue. 5. *Il a acheté la cage* = He (has) bought the cage.

Practice 12.2

1. *Marie (s) des provisions (o)* 2. *Le gâteau (s) elle (s)* 3. *La police (s) le criminel (o)* 4. *Le livre (s) je (s)*
5. *Tu (s) le match (o)*

Practice 12.3

1. *Il les mange* = He eats them. 2. *Nous le regardons* = We watch it. 3. *Mon frère l'a acheté* = My brother (has) bought it. 4. *Il va le lire très vite* = He is going to read it very quickly. 5. *Moi, je les préfère* = I prefer them.

Practice 12.4

1. *Je le vois souvent.* 2. *Sa mère les vend.* 3. *La télé? Ils la regardent beaucoup.* 4. *Le billet? Il l'a payé au guichet.* 5. *Le whisky? Elle ne le boit pas.*

Practice 13.1
1. *une casserole* 2. *des haricots.* 3. *une leçon* 4. *elle commence* 5. *ça casse* 6. *les Français* 7. *vous menacez* 8. *nous commençons*

Practice 13.2
1. *Noël* 2. *la maison* 3. *Anaïs Anaïs* 4. *Joëlle* 5. *une moitié* 6. *la moelle*

Practice 13.3
Les examens sont terminés et je peux passer la fête de Noël avec mon frère et sa fiancée. Programme d'activités: ciné, disco, arrivée de son corres français Gaël. Une bonne façon de se détendre!

Practice 14.1
1. *masque* √ 2. *voisin* √ 3. *programme* ? 4. *astrologue* √ 5. *Japon* √ 6. *privilège* √ 7. *crabe* ? 8. *bus* √ 9. *mètre* √ 10. *paravent* √ 11. *manteau* √ 12. *alibi* √

Practice 14.2
1. *inscription* √ 2. *bouche* √ 3. *plante* √ 4. *rage* ? 5. *journée* √ 6. *distance* ? 7. *Afrique* √ 8. *statue* √ 9. *chatte* √ 10. *couverture* √ 11. *chambre* ? 12. *essence* √

Practice 14.3
I looked at the first page of my cookery book. I found a recipe for mussels, prepared sailors' style.

Practice 14.4
Pour commencer je fais la grasse matinée jusqu'à dix heures et demie. Après le petit déjeuner, je prends le bus pour aller à la piscine. Je fais de la natation jusqu'à midi et demi avec une très jolie fille. Puis je retrouve ma copine, et nous allons prendre un verre ensemble. Plus tard je mange un sandwich avec ma fiancée, et je la laisse pour aller regarder un film avec la petite amie de mon voisin. C'est une personne très séduisante, pour qui j'ai une grande amitié. Ensuite, je prends le diner chez la cousine de ma mère. Elle est mûre et toujours charmante. Finalement je rentre chez moi et je passe la soirée avec ma femme. Une journée bien intéressante!

Practice 15.1
1. *C'était un hôtel confortable.* 2. *Pas mal, il y avait une piscine énorme.* 3. *Non, parce que je n'aime pas l'eau froide.* 4. *Non, je déteste la nourriture espagnole.* 5. *Je ne sais pas, j'ai parlé seulement avec des garçons anglais.* 6. *Non, l'été prochain je voudrais aller dans un pays intéressant.*

Practice 15.2
1. *Voici Médor, c'est mon gros chien brun.* 2. *Voici Zigzag, c'est mon long serpent jaune.*
3. *Voici Jeannot, c'est mon grand lapin noir.* 4. *Voici Bulle, c'est mon vieux poisson rouge.*
5. *Voici Roland, c'est mon beau rat sympathique.* 6. *Voici Sacha, c'est mon autre chat chamarré.*

Practice 15.3
1. his clean socks 2. his own socks 3. a former palace 4. his dear aunt 5. his only day off

Practice 15.4
1. *lundi dernier* 2. *un village tranquille* 3. *un mauvais repas* 4. *un jeune chanteur* 5. *le pauvre chien* 6. *le haut bâtiment* 7. *mon petit frère* 8. *son chat noir* 9. *le seul taxi* 10. *ton/votre propre appartement*

Practice 15.5
1. *les monuments historiques* 2. *les jeunes enfants* 3. *la cuisine régionale* 4. *les matchs passionnants* 5. *la semaine prochaine* 6. *une chatte noire* 7. *des appartements chers* 8. *un grand repas*

Practice 15.6

Il a organisé une grande fête, avec beaucoup de musique moderne et un énorme gâteau avec une belle décoration. Je portais mon jean neuf et mes baskets blanches. Comme cadeau, j'ai acheté un nouveau CD et une jolie carte. Nous avons fait un grand bruit, et la vieille voisine, qui n'est pas une personne gentille, nous a dit d'arrêter notre bonne soirée. Quel dommage!

Practice 15.7

1. *une belle journée* 2. *un bel endroit* 3. *un beau château* 4. *le vieux grand-père* 5. *la vieille maison*
6. *les vieux grands-parents* 7. *le vieil homme* 8. *le nouvel horaire* 9. *la nouvelle élève* 10. *un nouveau film.*

Practice 15.8

Les éléphants sont plus utiles que les moustiques. Les éléphants sont aussi stupides que les moustiques. Les éléphants sont moins légers que les moustiques. Les éléphants sont plus grands que les moustiques. Les éléphants sont moins énervants que les moustiques. Les éléphants sont aussi féroces que les moustiques. Les éléphants sont meilleurs que les moustiques.

Practice 15.9

1. *Non, l'éléphant est l'animal le moins petit.* 2. *Non, le moustique est l'insecte le moins agréable.*
3. *Non, l'éléphant est la créature la plus patiente.* 4. *Non, le moustique est la créature la moins grande.*
5. *Non, l'éléphant est la bête la plus bizarre.* 6. *Non, l'éléphant est le meilleur pour travailler.*

Practice 16.1

Toute cette semaine j'ai beaucoup travaillé. Pour cette raison, j'ai décidé d'aller au centre de loisirs. A cet endroit on peut choisir toutes sortes d'activités. Ces possibilités permettent de bien apprécier ce complexe multisports.

Practice 16.2

Fabien: Oui, avec mes copains et mon frère.
Sylvain: Et ton frère, il a pris sa propre voiture?
Fabien: Non, il a pris la voiture de ma mère.
Sylvain: Tu es allé à ton club préféré?
Fabien: Oui, et il y avait ma chanteuse favorite, accompagnée de son groupe.

Practice 16.3

1. *son anorak* 2. *son anorak* 3. *ton ami Mustapha* 4. *ton amie Fatima* 5. *ses amis* 6. *ses yeux* 7. *son nez* 8. *mes frères et (mes) sœurs*

Practice 16.4

1. *notre salon* 2. *nos chambres* 3. *notre jardin* 4. *notre cuisine* 5. *nos garages*

Practice 16.5

1. *votre hôtel* 2. *votre vol* 3. *vos activités* 4. *votre piscine* 5. *vos passeports*

Practice 16.6

1. *leurs parents* 2. *leur mère* 3. *leur sœur* 4. *leurs cousin(e)s* 5. *leurs oncle*

Practice 16.7

Ah, bon? Dedans il y a votre porte-monnaie? Ah, bon? Et aussi votre carte d'identité? Ah, bon? Et puis une photo de vos chats? Ah, bon? Egalement vos cachets d'aspirine? Ah, bon? Et enfin votre carnet d'adresses?

Practice 16.8

Tout pour tes loisirs d'été, tout pour ton sport favori! Ton équipement, tes cours avec moniteurs, ton assurance, ta carte info. Achète ici ton billet, c'est 50 € seulement.

Practice 17.1

1. *calmement* = calmly 2. *réellement* = really 3. *traditionnellement* = traditionally 4. *constamment* = constantly 5. *heureusement* = happily/fortunately

Practice 17.2

1. *C'est un train rapide, il voyage rapidement/vite* = It's a fast/quick train, it travels fast/quickly. 2. *Le repas était bon, nous avons bien mangé* = The meal was good, we ate well. 3. *Cette histoire est récente, c'est arrivé récemment* = This story is recent, it happened recently. 4. *Le service est régulier, les bus arrivent régulièrement* = The service is regular, the buses arrive regularly. 5. *Les enfants sont gentils, ils jouent gentiment* = The children are nice, they are playing nicely. 6. *Je suis malade, je ne vais pas bien* = I am ill, I am not well. 7. *Avec ce médicament, je vais aller mieux* = With this medicine, I am going to be better. 8. *C'est bien le train pour le Stade de France, n'est-ce pas?* = This is the train for the Stade de France, isn't it? 9. *Il y a eu un accident tragique, l'assistante du magicien est morte tragiquement* = There was a tragic accident, the magician's assistant died tragically.

Practice 18.1

1. *elle s'amuse* = she enjoys herself/she has a good time 2. *vous vous habillez* = you get dressed 3. *je me repose* = I have a rest 4. *ils se rasent* = they have a shave 5. *nous nous dépêchons* = we hurry 6. *on se douche* = we/you/they have a shower

Practice 18.2

1. *Elle se lève, puis elle lève le bébé.* 2. *Elle se lave, puis elle lave le bébé.* 3. *Elle s'habille, puis elle habille le bébé.* 4. *Elle se promène et elle promène le bébé.* 5. *Elle se change, puis elle change le bébé.* 6. *Elle couche le bébé, et enfin elle se couche.*

Practice 18.3

1. *Le chat et l'oiseau se regardent.* 2. *Myriam et Philippe se voient sur leurs portables.* 3. *David et Claire s'envoient un mail.* 4. *Le 1er janvier, les gens se disent: 'Bonne année!'* 5. *Mark et Linda s'écrivent une carte.*

Practice 19.1

1. *on finit* 2. *Suzanne grandit* 3. *les jeunes sortent* 4. *Ali et Khaled dorment* 5. *tu grossis* 6. *le jardin verdit* 7. *je vieillis* 8. *les plantes jaunissent*

Practice 19.2

1. *je tiens* = I hold 2. *elles viennent* = they come 3. *il tient* = he holds 4. *nous venons* = we come 5. *vous tenez* = you hold

Practice 19.3

1. *il /on sait* = he/one knows (how to) 2. *vous devez* = you have to 3. *nous savons* = we know (how to) 4. *ils doivent* = they have to 5. *vous savez* = you know (how to)

Practice 19.4

1. *elle veut* = she wants 2. *vous voulez* = you want 3. *je peux* = I am able to/can 4. *on veut* = one wants 5. *ils peuvent* = they are able to/can

Practice 19.5

1. *ils offrent* = they offer/give 2. *vous offrez* = you offer/give 3. *nous ouvrons* = we open 4. *ils ouvrent* = they open 5. *elles offrent* = they offer/give

Practice 19.6

1. *Vous entendez le bébé qui pleure?* = Do/can you hear the baby crying? 2. *Loïc descend du train* = Loïc gets off (literally: comes down from) the train 3. *Ici on vend toutes sortes de souvenirs* = Here they sell (literally: one sells) all kinds of souvenirs. 4. *Les stars répondent aux questions de l'interviewer* = The stars reply to the interviewer's questions. 5. *Nous t'attendons devant la gare* = We are waiting for you outside (literally: in front of) the station. 6. *Je n'entends pas bien la musique sur mon lecteur CD* = I don't/can't hear the music properly on my CD player. 7. *Tu vends ta voiture?* = Are you selling your car? 8. *Ma copine descend la piste de ski à toute vitesse* = My friend comes down the ski slope at great (literally: at all) speed.

Practice 19.7

Axelle: *Où es-tu?*
Salomé: *Je suis au supermarché, et toi?*
Axelle: *Moi, je prends le petit déjeuner.*
Salomé: *Tu veux faire un pique-nique cet après-midi?*
Axelle: *Pourquoi pas? Il fait beau.*
Salomé: *D'accord. Je viens te prendre chez toi à onze heures.*

Practice 19.8

1. *Elle dit qu'elle est fatiguée* = She say she is tired. 2. *Tu dis qu'il m'aime?* = Are you saying he loves me? 3. *Mon père boit trop de bière* = My father drinks too much beer. 4. *Qu'est-ce que vous dites? Parlez plus fort!* = What are you saying? Speak louder! 5. *On dit que la grammaire française est difficile* = They say (literally: one says) that French grammar is difficult. 6. *Nous ne buvons pas d'alcool* = We don't drink (any) alcohol.

Practice 20.1

1. *Ce matin je joue au tennis, et demain matin aussi je jouerai au tennis* = I shall play tennis.
2. *Aujourd'hui à midi on mange une pizza, et demain midi encore on mangera une pizza* = We shall eat a pizza. 3. *Cet après-midi nous regardons un film, et demain après-midi aussi nous regarderons un film* = We shall watch a film. 4. *Ce soir je retrouve mes copains, et demain soir également je retrouverai mes copains* = I shall meet my friends. 5. *Puis on se couche vers dix heures, et la même chose demain, on se couchera vers dix heures* = We shall go to bed at about ten o'clock.

Practice 20.2

1. *ils/elles comprendront* 2. *nous choisirons* 3. *je sortirai* 4. *tu grandiras/vous grandirez* 5. *elle boira* 6. *il répondra*

Practice 20.3

1. *tu devras* 2. *il aura* 3. *elle saura* 4. *je pourrai* 5. *nous viendrons* 6. *vous ferez*

Practice 20.4

1. *aller* 2. *venir* 3. *avoir* 4. *voir* 5. *faire* 6. *devoir* 7. *savoir* 8. *pouvoir*

Practice 20.5

Antoine: *J'irai en Bretagne avec des copains.*
Fred: *Vous serez combien?*
Antoine: *Il y aura Michel, Pierre et moi, donc nous serons trois. Malheureusement, Maryse ne pourra pas venir. Elle m'a dit qu'elle n'aura pas d'argent et qu'elle devra travailler pour son père.*
Fred: *C'est vrai, ces vacances seront chères, non?*
Antoine: *Non, pas du tout, tu verras. Nous ferons des économies, donc on pourra louer une voiture. Nous aurons nos sacs de couchage, alors nous pourrons faire du camping.*
Fred: *Tu devras économiser beaucoup?*
Antoine: *Oui, en effet. Mais dis donc!*

Fred:	*Quoi?*
Antoine:	*Est-ce que tu seras libre au mois de juillet?*
Fred:	*Oh, je ne sais pas.*
Antoine:	*Quand est-ce que tu le sauras? J'ai quelque chose à te proposer.*
Fred:	*Quoi?*
Antoine:	*Tu viendras en France avec nous?*
Fred:	*Non merci, je voudrai me reposer chez moi!*

Practice 20.6

1. *L'année prochaine, elle aura dix-huit ans* = Next year, she will be eighteen. 2. *Ils ne pourront pas l'accompagner parce qu'ils n'ont pas d'argent* = They will not be able to go with her because they have no money. 3. *Si tu travailles pendant dix heures, tu seras fatigué* = If you work for ten hours, you will be tired. 4. *Ce soir, nous verrons/regarderons le film au Rex* = This evening/tonight, we will see/watch the film at the Rex. 5. *Vous viendrez au concert avec moi?* = Will you come to the concert with me?

Practice 20.7

1. *Je voyagerai en Eurostar.* 2. *Ça sera rapide.* 3. *Je logerai dans un hôtel au centre-ville.* 4. *Avec ma famille, nous visiterons beaucoup de choses.* 5. *Nous mangerons des spécialités françaises.* 6. *Nous prendrons le métro.* 7. *Nous verrons la Tour Eiffel.* 8. *Nous pourrons parler français.* 9. *Mes parents voudront visiter des musées.* 10. *J'espère qu'il fera beau.*

Practice 21.1

1. *tu as aimé* = you (have) liked 2. *on a mangé* = one (ate/has) eaten 3. *j'ai préféré* = I (have) preferred 4. *vous avez admiré* = you (have) admired 5. *ils ont chanté* = they have sung/they sang 6. *elle a écouté* = she (has) listened (to)

Practice 21.2

1. *Angèle a voyagé en train.* 2. *Vous avez envoyé un mail.* 3. *Les Dawson ont habité Paris.* 4. *Nous avons parlé français.* 5. *On a apprécié le confort.* 6. *J'ai adoré les croissants.*

Practice 21.3

1. *elle a couru* 2. *nous avons pu* 3. *il a eu* 4. *tu as/vous avez ouvert* 5. *j'ai fini*

Practice 21.4

1. *j'ai répondu* 2. *ils/elles ont cru* 3. *tu as/vous avez dit* 4. *elle a été* 5. *nous avons attendu* 6. *tu as/vous avez écrit* 7. *il a pris* 8. *j'ai mis*

Practice 21.5

1. *Il a couru jusqu'à la gare.* = He ran to the station 2. *Nous avons dit: 'Bon anniversaire!'* = We said: 'Happy birthday!' 3. *Ils ont voulu aller en ville.* = They wanted to go to town 4. *Elle a pris son sac.* = She took her bag 5. *Tu as eu froid.* = You were cold 6. *On a fait du ski.* = We went skiing

Practice 22.1

1. *Nous nous sommes dépêchés pour prendre le train.* = We hurried to catch the train. 2. *Mes amis sont arrivés en retard.* = My friends arrived late. 3. *Hier soir, elles ont mangé au restaurant.* = Last night, they ate out (in a restaurant). 4. *Tu es parti sans dire au revoir.* = You left without saying goodbye. 5. *Vous avez voyagé en avion?* = Did you fly (travel by plane)?

Practice 22.2

1. *L'homme a monté l'escalier* = The man went up the stairs.
2. *Mon frère est monté jusqu'au premier étage* = My brother went up to the first floor.
3. *Nous sommes rentrés chez nous* = We went back home.
4. *Tu as rentré tes affaires?* = Did you bring your things back in?
5. *Elle s'est regardée dans le miroir* = She looked at herself in the mirror.

6. *Elle a regardé ses photos de vacances* = She looked at her holiday photos.
7. *Je me suis levée quand mon réveil a sonné* = I got up when my alarm clock rang.
8. *J'ai levé mon petit frère* = I got my little brother up.

Practice 22.3

Quand je suis entrée j'ai remarqué un jeune homme très beau. Il m'a souri et, je ne sais pas pourquoi, je me suis approchée de lui. 'Je vous ai vu quelque part, n'est-ce pas?' ai-je dit. Il a hésité un instant, puis il a répondu: 'Oui, nous nous sommes rencontrés la semaine dernière chez Nicolas. J' y suis allé avec ma petite amie Ludivine, mais nous nous sommes disputés quand elle a vu que je vous regardais. J' ai voulu vous parler, mais elle s'est fâchée et elle m'a abandonné.

Practice 22.4

Je lui ai dit: 'Pourquoi est-ce que vous ne m'avez pas demandé de danser quand votre copine est partie?' Il a rougi, puis il s'est décidé: 'Est-ce que vous avez fait du saut à l'élastique? C'est passionnant.' Nous nous sommes regardés, l'amour dans les yeux. Et voilà comment notre histoire a commencé!

Practice 23.1

1. Perf.: one occasion 2. Imp.: background information; Perf.: one occasion 3. Imp.: background information; Perf.: one occasion 4. Imp.: background information; Perf.: one occasion 5. Perf.: finished action 6. Imp.: background information; Imp.: regularly in past 7. Imp.: regularly in past; Imp: background information 8. Perf.: one occasion; Perf.: one occasion

Practice 23.2

1. *tu donnais* = you were giving/you used to give/you gave 2. *il buvait* = he was drinking/he used to drink/he drank 3. *nous prenions* = we were taking/we used to take/we took 4. *vous choisissiez* = you were choosing/you used to choose/you chose 5. *ils vendaient* = they were selling/they used to sell/they sold

Practice 23.3

1. être - *Elles étaient contentes.* 2. finir = *Ils finissaient leur match.* 3. aller = *Tu allais à la fête?* 4. préférer = *Tout le monde préférait les vacances au travail.* 5. faire = *Je ne faisais pas de ski.* 6. vouloir = *Ma voisine voulait nous inviter.* 7. aller = *Vous alliez au centre-ville.* 8. prendre = *Je prenais le métro.* 9. donner = *Les chanteurs donnaient un concert tous les soirs.* 10. être = *Pourquoi est-ce que tu étais à Lyon cet été?* 11. répondre = *Vous ne répondiez pas.* 12. se préparer = *Daniel se préparait à toute vitesse.* 13. monter = *On montait à la Tour Eiffel.* 14. boire = *Nous buvions du Champagne.* 15. devoir = *Je devais rentrer chez moi.*

Practice 23.4

J'ai passé dix jours chez mon correspondant, qui habitait en Bretagne. La nourriture était excellente, et j'ai bu du vin pour la première fois. Il était très fort!
Chaque jour, nous avons fait une excursion dans la région. Madame Beraud conduisait plus vite que ma mère. Elle m'a montré beaucoup d'endroits intéressants. Un jour, nous sommes allés au Mont Saint Michel. Il y avait beaucoup de touristes.
Après dix jours, j'ai dû rentrer en Angleterre, et j'étais un peu triste. Pendant mon séjour, j'ai pris beaucoup de photos et, le jour de mon départ, la famille m'a offert du vin. Les bouteilles étaient lourdes! Heureusement j'ai passé la douane sans problème, mais quand je suis arrivé chez moi, j'ai découvert qu'une des bouteilles était cassée, et que tous mes vêtements étaient tachés.

Practice 23.5

Il était neuf heures du soir et il faisait nuit. Madame Marquet, une vieille dame plutôt sourde qui vivait seule, a décidé d'acheter des provisions au petit magasin qui se trouvait en face de chez elle. Elle est sortie très vite de son appartement parce que le magasin était sur le point de fermer. A cette heure, il n'y avait pas beaucoup de circulation d'habitude, donc elle n'a pas regardé pour voir s'il y avait des voitures qui s'approchaient. Elle a commencé à traverser la rue. Elle n'a pas entendu le moteur d'un gros camion qui roulait assez vite vers elle ...

Practice 23.6

Madame Marquet était au milieu de la rue quand le camion est arrivé. A la dernière seconde, le camionneur, qui était fatigué, a vu Madame Marquet. Il a essayé de freiner, mais c'était trop tard! Le camion est entré en collision avec la pauvre dame, qui est tombée et est restée immobile. Le camionneur, qui avait peur de perdre son emploi si on pensait qu'il était responsable de l'accident, est parti sans s'arrêter. On a trouvé madame Marquet le lendemain matin – morte.

Practice 24.1

1. *Elle a passé de bonnes vacances?* 2. *Tu partiras avec elle l'année prochaine?* 3. *Tes parents seront d'accord?* 4. *Vous resterez au même endroit?* 5. *Je pourrai venir aussi?*

Practice 24.2

1. *Avec qui est-ce que tu y es allé?* 2. *Combien est-ce que vous avez payé?* 3. *Qu'est-ce que c'était comme film?* 4. *Pourquoi est-ce que tu préfères les films d'horreur?* 5. *Quand est-ce que vous êtes allés au cinéma?*

Practice 24.3

1. *Quelle équipe est-ce que tu supportes?* 2. *Comment est-ce qu'ils s'entraînent?* 3. *Quand est-ce que le prochain match sera?* 4. *Où est-ce qu'ils vont jouer?* 5. *Qui est-ce qui va gagner?*

Practice 24.4

1. Cannot be inverted 2. *Angélique voudra-t-elle sortir avec moi?* 3. *Suis-je assez charmant pour elle?* 4. *Que va-t-on faire?* 5. *Ai-je assez d'argent pour l'emmener manger chez Maxim?*

Practice 24.5

1. *Combien de places vont-ils réserver?* 2. *Pourquoi Mylène n' aime-t-elle pas Cédric?* 3. *Avec qui sort-elle ce soir?* 4. *Que va-t-il faire pendant les grandes vacances?* 5. *Comment est-ce que je peux apprendre la grammaire française?*

Practice 25.1

1. *Les footballeurs ne sont pas toujours très intelligents.* 2. *Nous ne sommes pas allés faire du ski à Paris.* 3. *Je n'irai pas en vacances sur la lune l'année prochaine.* 4. *L'année dernière, ils n'ont pas traversé le désert en bateau.* 5. *Il ne fait pas plus chaud en Suède qu'au Mexique.*

Practice 25.2

1. *Où es-tu sortie le week-end dernier?* – (c) *Je ne suis allée nulle part.* 2. *Comment as-tu passé le temps?* – (b) *Je n'ai rien fait.* 3. *Avec qui as-tu discuté?* – (f) *Je n'ai parlé à personne.* 4. *Qui est-ce que tu as rencontré?* – (e) *Je n'ai vu que mes parents.* 5. *Tu es contente de ta vie?* – (a) *Non, elle n'est pas idéale.* 6. *Tu as encore des copains?* – (d) *Non, je n'ai plus d'amis.*

Practice 25.3

1. *Personne* 2. *Rien* 3. *Jamais* 4. *Personne* 5. *Rien*

Practice 25.4

1. *Tous les chemins ne mènent pas à Bruxelles!* 2. *On ne trouve jamais rien à faire.* 3. *Personne n'est sympathique.* 4. *La cuisine n'est jamais délicieuse.* 5. *On ne trouve de restaurants nulle part.* 6. *Ils ne servent que des moules-frites.* 7. *Il n'y a pas de musées intéressants et pas de monuments historiques non plus/Il n'y a ni musées intéressants, ni monuments historiques.* 8. *Quand on a visité la Belgique, on ne veut plus y retourner.*

Practice 26.1

1. Subj. – Dir. Obj. 2. Subj. – Ind. Obj. 3. Subj. – Ind. Obj. – Subj. – Dir. Obj. 4. Subj. – Subj. 5. Subj. – Dir. Obj. – Dir. Obj.

Practice 26.2

1. *Edith choisit un CD, puis elle l'achète.* 2. *Les enfants disent 'bon anniversaire' à leur mère, puis ils lui donnent des fleurs.* 3. *Vous voulez ce magazine? Vous pouvez le prendre, j'ai fini de le lire.* 4. *Où as-tu trouvé ce joli pull? Je vais te l'emprunter, si tu veux bien!* 5. *Isabelle n'a pas dit à ses parents où elle sortait. Elle ne leur a pas dit la vérité.*

Practice 26.3

1. *Elle ne l'a pas regardé.* 2. *Mes amis m'ont téléphoné et nous avons discuté.* 3. *Pour son anniversaire ils lui écriront une carte.* 4. *Cédric m'apporte toujours quelque chose quand il vient ici.* 5. *Préfères- tu venir avec nous à la piscine?*

Practice 26.4

1. *Elles sont les comédies, qui lui plaisent beaucoup.* 2. *Il lui dit de lire ou de jouer avec son frère.* 3. *Ils ne l'écoutent pas.* 4. *Quand il vient, ils leur téléphonent. Ils leur demandent de venir.* 5. *Ils viennent les chercher.*

Practice 26.5

1. *Elle lui a envoyé une lettre.* 2. *Elle l'a envoyé aux magasins.* 3. *Elle leur cuisine toujours un repas.* 4. *Elle les cuisine toujours très bien.* 5. *Nous lui avons acheté un nouveau CD.* 6. *Nous l'avons acheté à l'animalerie.* 7. *Ils lui apporteront un nouveau jouet.* 8. *Ils l'apporteront chez nous.* 9. *Je vais leur prêter ce livre.* 10. *Je vais les prêter à ma copine/à mon amie.*

Practice 26.6

1. *'C'est confortable chez nous!'* 2. *'Viens à côté de moi!'* 3. *'Il est beau, lui!'* 4. *'Elle est super, elle!'* 5. *'Et toi, comment t'appelles-tu?'*

Practice 26.7

1. *Combien d'argent as-tu apporté?* (b) *J'en ai apporté beaucoup.* = I (have) brought a lot. 2. *Est-ce qu'il fait de la planche à voile?* (c) *Seulement quand il y a du vent.* = Only when there is wind. 3. *Est-ce qu'il aime les chats?* (e) *Non, il en a peur!* = No, he is afraid of them. 4. *Habite-t-il à Paris?* (a) *Oui, il y loue un appartement.* = Yes, he rents a flat there. 5. *Il y a des tas d'exercices dans ce livre?* (d) *Oui, il y en a trop!* = Yes, there are too many!

Practice 26.8

1. *Moi, j'y suis arrivée avant-hier.* 2. *Moi, j'en ai deux.* 3. *J'aime y aller aussi.* 4. *Oui, je voudrais bien les rencontrer.* 5. *Oui, je vais leur demander.* 6. *Oui, nous ne l'avons pas encore vu.* 7. *J'espère les passer ici.* 8. *Super! Nous nous verrons, j'espère.* 9. *Oui, et tu m'écriras aussi!* 10. *Merci, et tu peux venir chez moi aussi.*

Practice 26.9

1. *Je te présente madame Chirac. Elle est ma voisine.* ⇒ *Je te présente madame Chirac qui est ma voisine.* 2. *Il mange le poulet. Elle l'a préparé.* ⇒ *Il mange le poulet qu'elle a préparé.* 3. *Nicole se décide pour les vacances en camping. Elles sont moins chères.* ⇒ *Nicole se décide pour les vacances en camping qui sont moins chères.* 4.*Tu ne vas pas au cinéma Panécran? Il est tout près.* ⇒ *Tu ne vas pas au cinéma Panécran qui est tout près?* 5. *Où est le journal? Tu l'as acheté ce matin.* ⇒ *Où est le journal que tu as acheté ce matin?*

Practice 26.10

C'est un nouveau modèle qui est très confortable. Il a des boutons qui sont en métal, et des poches que je trouve bien pratiques. Le premier jean que je voulais était trop grand, mais le vendeur, que je connais et qui est très aimable, m'en a apporté un autre qui était plus petit. Ma sœur a acheté le même pour aller avec le pull qu'elle a acheté récemment.

Practice 26.11

It's a new model that is very comfortable. It has metal buttons (that are made of metal), and pockets that I find very convenient. The first (pair of) jeans (that) I wanted was (were) too big, but the assistant, whom I know and who is very helpful, brought me another (pair) that was (were) smaller. My sister bought the same ones to go with the jumper (that) she bought recently.

'*qui*' can be translated by 'that' or 'who'; '*que/qu*' can be translated by 'that' or 'whom'.

Practice 26.12

1. *Est-ce que les explications étaient claires?* (a) *Oui, tout était très clair.* (b) *En général, pas mal.* (c) *Non, absolument pas. C'était confus.*

2. *As-tu trouvé les exercices faciles?* (a) *Oui, assez faciles.* (b) *Oui, beaucoup trop faciles pour moi.* (c) *Non, je n'ai pas pu les faire.*

3. *Est-ce qu'il y avait assez d'exercices?* (a) *Oui, le nombre juste.* (b) *Non, trop. C'était vraiment ennuyeux.* (c) *Non, je veux deux fois plus d'exercices.*

4. *Qu'est-ce que tu as pensé des dessins?* (a) *Ils étaient amusants.* (b) *Ils étaient plutôt stupides, pour les jeunes enfants.* (c) *Je n'ai pas vraiment remarqué les dessins.*

5. *Est-ce que tu recommanderas ce livre?* (a) *Oui, certainement, à mes copains/mon copain.* (b) *Non, c'est une perte de temps.* (c) *Non, la grammaire française est trop difficile.*

Et maintenant, bonne chance!